THE CROSS

AND THE

TENT PEG

HOW JESUS RETRACED JAEL'S STORY

THE CROSS
AND THE
TENT PEG

· JULIE WALSH ·

ISBN: 978-0-578-41365-5

To the glory of Jesus Christ

CONTENTS

INTRODUCTION

Scholars have seen intertextual references within Jesus' crucifixion and resurrection narratives in the form of quotes, allusions, and echoes from the Old Testament. Yet none have discovered a coherent *narrative pattern* connecting the events with any story in the Old Testament. This book will show, however, that in fact all four Gospels' accounts closely follow the narrative sequence of events of the Jael story. Moreover, throughout this study, the Jael narrative in Judg 4 and the Song of Deborah in Judg 5 will be proved to initially fulfill the *protoevangelium* of Gen 3:15 through a literalistic fulfillment. This reveals the culmination of the redemptive thread of promise in Gen 3:15 for the world as *to* and *through* Woman. The resulting metalepsis created by the fulfillment narrative pattern in the Gospels in turn alludes to the Gospel writers' beliefs about the atonement created by the death and resurrection of Jesus Christ.

The Significance of this Book

Theologians have recognized little intertextual evidence of an explicit apologetic for the death and resurrection of Jesus in the Gospels. This seems peculiar, given how prevalent references to the Old Testament are in the New Testament, with close to 2000 quotes, allusions, and echoes. The Gospels' similar accounts of the crucifixion and resurrection, however, have not been analyzed extensively in terms of a possible larger intertextual narrative pattern. Such a narrative pattern has been uncovered by Steve Moyise in the Book of Revelation with its author "following fairly precisely the sequence of events in the Book of Ezekiel."[1] Another example given by Jeannine Brown is of Jesus being compared and contrasted to Israel in his going through the waters in his baptism (Exod 14:21-22), being pronounced God's son (Exod 4:22-23), and then being led into the wilderness to be tested (Exod 14-32).[2] This study seeks to answer the question of whether there is a similar Old Testament narrative that aligns with the New Testament crucifixion and resurrection narratives.

According to John Ronning, the narrative of Jael may be one such story. In his recent book, *The Jewish Targums and John's Logos Theology*, Ronning suggests:

---

1. Ezek 37:10 and Rev 20:4, Ezek 37:21 and Rev 20:4, Ezek 38:2-16 and Rev 20:8, Ezek 38:22 and Rev 20:9, Ezek 39:4 and 19:21, Ezek 40:2 and 21:10, Ezek 40:5 and Rev 21:15, Ezek 43:12 and Rev 22:1-2, Ezek 48:30-34 and Rev 21:12-13. Steve Moyise, "Dialogical Intertextuality," in *Exploring Intertextuality: Diverse Strategies for New Testament Interpretation of Texts*, ed. B. J. Oropeza and Steve Moyise (Eugene, OR: Cascade Books, 2016), 6-7.

2. Jeannine K. Brown, "Metalepsis," in *Exploring Intertextuality: Diverse Strategies for New Testament Interpretation of Texts*, ed. B. J. Oropeza and Steve Moyise (Eugene, OR: Cascade Books, 2016), 32.

The crucifixion appears to be a total and final defeat, yet the reality is quite the opposite. The first promise of salvation in the Bible is the Lord's statement to the serpent: "He shall strike you on the head" (Gen 3:15). In several places in the OT, we see what could be called "literalistic" fulfillments of this ancient promise, as one of the "offspring of the serpent" meets his end in such a way as to remind us of this promise (though the promise itself is not to be fulfilled in literal terms). For example, Jael, the wife of Heber the Kenite, drove a tent peg through the skull of Sisera (Judg 4-5). David defeated Goliath with a blow to the head (1 Sam 17).... All four Gospels tell us that Jesus was crucified at "the place of a skull" (Matt 27:33; Mark 15:22; Luke 23:33; John 19:17), and here again we can see a literalistic fulfillment of Gen 3:15, with the cross of Jesus driven into this "skull." In the midst of apparent defeat, we see what is actually a sign of victory over the world and the devil, the crushing of the serpent's head, as the feet of the Son of God are pierced.[3]

This reference to Jael's actions as having a similarity to the crucifixion would also supply a powerful meta-narrative with an apologetic for the Cross. In Ronning's 1997 dissertation on Gen 3:15 he expanded on this theme:

This skull was, so to speak, trodden on by Jesus as he walked to the place of his crucifixion. As the skull of Sisera on the ground was pierced by Jael's tent peg, into the ground, so the cross of Jesus pierced the "Place of the Skull;" its rocks were also split open by an earthquake (Matt 27:51; cf. Abimelech's fate, Jdg 9:53). At the same time, his feet

---

3. John Ronning, *The Jewish Targums and John's Logos Theology* (Grand Rapids, MI: Baker Academic, 2010), 141-42.

> were pierced, recalling literalistically Gen 3:15e, as well as
> Ps 22:17 (16).[4]

As tantalizing as these ideas are, Ronning does not further explore other possible correspondences between the narrative of Jael in Judg 4 and the Song of Deborah in Judg 5 with the Gospels' accounts of the crucifixion and resurrection. This study will show that in fact all four Gospels' accounts follow fairly precisely the narrative sequence of events of Jael's actions and storyline, which can be interpreted as the initial fulfillment of the Gen 3:15 promise.

The resulting intertextual narrative pattern discovered in this project discloses some of the Gospel writers' understandings of the atonement and the resurrection. These can influence atonement models, affect ecclesiology, sociology, ethics, missiology, biblical anthropology, and much more.

Scope

This study explores the Jael narrative as being an intertextual reference behind the Gospels' accounts of the crucifixion and resurrection explicitly. Therefore, it will not consider the apostle Paul's writings concerning this subject, nor any of the other New Testament authors. Likewise, there will not be space to analyze each Gospel for foreshadowing this story, although some allusions will be considered. Not all possible intertextuality and literary approaches will be used to illumine the highlighted passages, either. The atonement models suggested by the analysis

---

4. John L. Ronning, "The Curse on the Serpent (Genesis 3:15) in Biblical Theology and Hermeneutics" (PhD diss., Westminster Theological Seminary, 1997): 352, accessed September 4, 2017, ProQuest Dissertations Publishing.

will also only be mentioned briefly for further study. Further, anthropologies and feminine epistemologies that do not have the exegesis of biblical texts as their main starting point will not be considered. It is also impossible to give all early church references to Jael or a full analysis of references to Judg 4 and 5 by the early church writers. This study will discuss, however, the story of Jael as the narrative pattern behind the Gospels' accounts of the crucifixion and resurrection of Jesus; and it will prove the texts to be closely connected through critical exploration of the research pertaining to exegesis, intertextuality, and theological analysis.

Background Material

Exploring the literature surrounding a possible fulfillment narrative pattern in the crucifixion and resurrection narratives in the Gospels discloses both scholars on intertextuality and those who have studied Jael as pertaining to Gen 3:15 or the Cross. The scholars focusing on intertextuality have analyzed how references function in the texts and what they communicate to their audience. Understanding this can provide clues as to what form intertextual references in the Gospels' crucifixion and resurrection narratives might take. With this knowledge— and given that this paper contends that the Jael story is one such intertextual reference—a dramatist and poet from the 17th century Spanish Golden Age will be highlighted to witness how he saw God glorified in the Jael narrative and song. Next, two scholars who understand the Jael story as a type of fulfillment of the Gen 3:15 promise will be examined to explore a possible reason why the Jael story would be behind the Gospel writers' understandings of Jesus' Passion. Given their conclusions, scholars who have written on how the Gen 3:15 promise has been fulfilled in Christ will be mentioned. Lastly, two church fathers who spoke about Jael's actions will be briefly mentioned, concluding the review of the literature.

Intertextual narrative patterns have previously been noted as being the back-story behind some of Rev 19-22 as well as the stories of Jesus' baptism and wilderness testing. Similarly, Sylvia Keesmaat sees allusions and echoes in Rom 8:8-39 retelling the Exodus narrative. When analyzing Keesmaat's work, Steve Moyise summarizes her findings as regards to intertextuality:

> (a) the Exodus story which Paul tells is one that has already been transformed by prophets such as Hosea, Isaiah and Jeremiah, and traditions such as Wisdom, Sirach, Baruch and Enoch;
>
> (b) the invasive action of God in Jesus Christ introduced a new element into the story, an unexpected twist in the plot;
>
> (c) all retelling of the past, as opposed to merely repeating it, involves an element of transformation (1999:233). Narrative intertextuality then emphasizes both the continuing role of a significant story, while also acknowledging that each new retelling is in some sense a reshaping of that story.[5]

Therefore, if Jael's story is an intertextual narrative reference behind the crucifixion and resurrection stories, Jael's story in Judges itself may be commenting on a different scriptural reference. Plus, references to Jael's story may also appear in the Latter

---

5. Steve Moyise, "Intertextuality and Biblical Studies: A Review," *Verbum et Ecclesia 23*, no. 2 (August 2002): 422, accessed June 23, 2018, https://www.researchgate.net/publication/267545243_Intertextuality_and_Biblical_Studies_A_Review.

Prophets and Writings. And since Jesus Christ is the fulfillment of all the promises of God in the Old Testament, his actions may supply a plot twist to that narrative, as Keesmaat sees.

Peter Mallen speaks about the issues involved specifically in narrative pattern intertextuality and suggests how to deal with their inherent subjectivity:

> One obvious problem with identifying allusions and narrative patterns is that they make only indirect or implicit reference to precursor texts. Readers may miss an intended allusion or alternatively perceive an allusion where one was not intended. Hence identification of allusions and narrative patterns will always involve a level of subjectivity. Since the presence of allusions cannot be "proved," it seems more helpful to qualify allusions by terms such as "probably," "plausible" and "possible." Various criteria have been proposed by scholars to limit the degree of subjectivity.[6]

Beyond qualifying narrative patterns with "probably," "plausible" and "possible," what Mallen arrives at in his study of the relationship between Luke and Isaiah is the importance of "the cumulative effect of multiple allusions and narrative patterns."[7] For instance, the audience may wonder about one allusion at the beginning of a story but be convinced of the narrative pattern intertextuality after many such echoes to the alluded to text.

Ziva Ben-Porat provides helpful terminology for these narrative patterns and an analysis of their structure.[8] When

---

6. Peter Mallen, *The Reading and Transformation of Isaiah in Luke-Acts* (London: T & T Clark, 2008), 24.

7. Mallen gives as an example of this narrative pattern intertextuality Lk. 1.5-25; cf. Gen. 16.1; 17.1; 15-19; 1 Sam. 1.1-20. Mallen, *Isaiah in Luke-Acts*, 24.

8. Ziva Ben-Porat, "The Poetics of Literary Allusion," *PTL: A Journal for Descriptive Poetics and Theory of Literature* 1 (1976): 105–128.

considering two texts together, Ben-Porat sees a *marker* and the *marked text* in Stage 1, saying, "The marker is always identifiable as an element or pattern belonging to another independent text."[9] This marker can be more familiar than the marked text itself, so Stage 2 involves recognizing the marked text. Stage 3 happens when there is recognition of the two texts and the interaction of them in the reader's mind causes a "modified version needed for the fuller interpretation of the alluding text."[10] Stage 4 occurs with the "activation of the evoked text, in an attempt to form maximal intertextual patterns," and this "further activation of elements is the particular aim for which the literary allusion is characteristically employed."[11] In other words, when recognized, the allusion causes the reader to meditate on the correspondence between the two texts and come to new ideas and conclusions. Richard Hays would call this the "poetic effect of metalepsis," where the powerful effect lies in the unstated or suppressed points of similarity between the two texts. The effect of metalepsis is what often exhorts the reader to action.[12] Ben-Porat's analysis is particularly beneficial for breaking down the flow of intertextual fulfillment narrative patterns. It can also illumine the motivation for any narrative pattern within the crucifixion and resurrection accounts besides the actual fulfillment of prophecy.

Two major new works examining the New Testament's intertextual references are books by Ben Witherington III and Richard Hays. In *Torah Old and New: Exegesis, Intertextuality,*

---

9. Ben-Porat, "The Poetics of Literary Allusion,"108.

10. Ibid., 110-11.

11. Ibid., 111.

12. Richard B. Hays, *Echoes of Scripture in the Gospels* (Waco, TX: Baylor University Press, 2016), 11.

and Hermeneutics, Witherington agrees with Hays that the Gospel of John uses a complex intertextual overlay of three images from Dan 7:13-14, Numbers 21, and Isaiah 52:13 in John 12:31-33 as prefigurations of the crucifixion and resurrection.[13] He also notes the combination citation in the passion narrative concerning the den of thieves in Luke 19:46 as from both Isaiah 56:7 and Jeremiah 7:11.[14] This opens up the possibility that there may be more than one allusion behind the Gospels' crucifixion and resurrection narratives, and even behind the more obvious quotations. Witherington also instructs,

> One of the more interesting observations that can be made from the outset is that while a prophecy, or the poetry of the Psalms, or even laws may be carefully quoted in the NT, often with citation formulas of various sorts to indicate a quotation is involved, **narrative material, on the other hand, is seldom directly quoted, nor are citation formulas regularly used to introduce the quotation. Rather stories tend to be summarized or paraphrased, and so recycled for other purposes and contexts.** ... *Quotations* are but the tip of the iceberg, and more often than not the material is being drawn on as **the true back-story to what the author wants to say now** about Jesus, his followers, and other relevant topics (emphasis added).[15]

This means that if the Gospels' accounts of the crucifixion and resurrection do allude to a narrative in the Old Testament, they will probably not quote directly from that narrative or use citation formulas, but may paraphrase and summarize it instead.

---

13. Ben Witherington III, *Torah Old and New: Exegesis, Intertextuality, and Hermeneutics* (Minneapolis: Fortress Press, 2018), 263-64.

14. Witherington, *Torah Old and New*, 15.

15. Ibid., 36-37.

In *Echoes of Scripture in the Gospels*, Richard Hays looks at each Gospel account separately and recognizes that the Evangelists see how Jesus is prefigured by Moses and the prophets, but nowhere does he contemplate places in the New Testament that may be allusions to Gen 3:15 or Jael's narrative in a larger intertextual narrative pattern.[16]

Looking to the world of 17th century poetry, Pedro Calderón de la Barca saw a confluence between the Cross, Jael, and Gen 3:15. Nancy Mayberry has examined Calderón's sacramental play ¿Quién hallará mujer fuerte? ("Who will Find/Discover the Strong Woman?") and stated that Calderón viewed Jael as a prefiguration of the Virgin Mother and also the Gen 3:15 woman.[17] Translated the seventh line of the play references Gen 3:15, saying that from an invincible woman, the word of Genesis says, the front will break the dragon, which Mayberry believes is due to the Vulgate's mistranslation of Gen 3:15.[18] The plays also has Sisera falling at Jael's feet, evoking both Lucifer's fall from heaven and Adam and Eve's fall in the garden.[19] Jael uses a hammer and nails, recalling the signs of the passion, and the prophet Deborah views Jael's actions as the supernatural sign that Jael is the woman promised in Genesis to trample the head of the dragon.[20]

Although many put the focus on Deborah, for Calderón Jael "is the one forecast in Genesis who would break the head of the devil. The latter is therefore accorded the garland, for her

---

16. Hays, *Echoes of Scripture in the Gospels*.

17. Nancy K. Mayberry, "The 'Strong Woman' in Calderón's *Autos*: The Exegetical and Iconographic Tradition of the Virgin Immaculate," *Bulletin of the Comediantes 49*, no. 2 (1997): 307-318, accessed June 23, 2018, https://muse.jhu.edu/article/390496/pdf, 307.

18. Mayberry, "The 'Strong Woman' in Calderón's *Autos*," 309.

19. Ibid., 311.

20. Ibid., 311.

feat was greater: Deborah saved her people, the Israelites, but Jael—in her role as the conqueror over the devil—is the prefiguration of the one whose obedience saved the whole world."[21] Mayberry also identifies that the strong women of the Old Testament Calderón discusses—Deborah, Jael, Abigail, Ruth and Rebekah—are not just prefigurations of Mary but "each is also represented as a strong, resourceful and able adversary, who defeats the ancient foe. Their iconographic representation as strong women is the figure of the woman trampling the head of the serpent."[22] Therefore, Calderón sees strong women of God defeating a serpent-figure as a recurring motif of the Old Testament.

Among scholars studying Gen 3:15 in particular, James Hamilton, John Ronning, Katherine Bushnell and Joseph Ratzinger are those most relevant to this study. James Hamilton looks at Gen 3:15 and draws up a thorough list of intertexual usage, but he does not prioritize the references he goes through to those that *most* represent the verbal and literary elements of Gen 3:15 to discover its meaning to its audience.[23] Hamilton sees the promise of the seed in Gen 3:15 as the one who would restore an Edenic state, yet he doesn't detail this state.[24] He does briefly question the possibility, however, that since the one who crushed the serpent's head did so at "the place of the skull," this may have later given rise to that as the name of the place where

---

21. Ibid., 312.

22. Ibid., 315.

23. James M. Hamilton, "The Skull Crushing Seed of the Woman: Inner-Biblical Interpretation of Genesis 3: 15," *Southern Baptist Journal of Theology 10*, no. 2 (2006): 30-54, accessed September 19, 2017, http://equip.sbts.edu/wp-content/uploads/2010/07/sbjt_102_sum06-hamilton.pdf.

24. Hamilton, "The Skull Crushing Seed of the Woman," 49n45.

the crucifixion happened.[25]

John Ronning goes further than Hamilton and attempts to discover how Gen 3:15 is interpreted throughout the Bible itself. He believes that Scripture indicates the two progenitors are figureheads for the true *spiritual* progenitors.[26] He explores what he terms "literalistic fulfillments" of Gen 3:15, for instance in Jael's and David's actions.[27] Likewise, Ronning sees a literalistic fulfillment of Gen 3:15 when Jesus is crucified at "the place of a skull," with the cross of Jesus driven into this "skull" and the feet of the Son of God are pierced.[28] Ronning sees allusions to the verse in the New Testament in Jn 3:14; Jn 8:38-47, 58; Ephesians 2; Gal 3:16 with the promised seed being Christ's; Rom 16:20 and Revelation 12, which he finds similar to the *Palestinian Tgs.* description of Gen 3:15. He also identifies who the "offspring of the serpent" are, stating,

> John is commonly accused of anti-Semitism because of his pejorative references to "the Jews" and especially because of the words of Jesus in John 8:44, "you are of your father the devil." However, "offspring of the serpent" is **simply a way of saying they are unregenerate**, which is the natural state of all people, not just Jews. Cain, the prototype of the offspring of the serpent, was obviously not Jewish (emphasis added).[29]

Ronning concludes that the Old Testament sees "figurative spiritual identification of the two seeds (one of faith and righteousness, one of unbelief and wickedness) and their respective

---

25. Ibid., 53n89.

26. Ronning, "The Curse on the Serpent," iii.

27. Ronning, *The Jewish Targums*, 141-2.

28. Ibid., 142.

29. Ronning, *The Jewish Targums*, 273.

progenitors (God, with Eve as figurehead, and an evil angelic being, with the snake as figurehead)."[30] However, the Scriptures rarely refer to Eve; instead, it is the offspring of a woman that is usually referred to. Finally, Ronning sees a riddle where the "he" doesn't have "her seed" as its antecedent and so replaces "the woman" with Christ in Gen 3:15 in his interpretation.[31] But this interpretation doesn't recognize that Christ should be viewed as the *offspring*, not the *woman*, since the Christ does the crushing of the Serpent as the offspring of the woman. Ronning also believes, problematically, the theme of Gen 3:15 to be the victory over *human* moral enemies and that "there must be an eschatological, 'crushing of the head' victory of the righteous over the wicked,"[32] whereas Gen 3:15 actually states that the offspring shall crush or strike the Serpent, not the Serpent's offspring.

Katharine C. Bushnell (1856-1946) also begins with Gen 3:15 and realizes that God's plan for the "new woman" in Jesus Christ is that a woman would not turn away to her husband, as did Eve, but remain loyal to God alone.[33] In Gen 3:15 Bushnell sees woman as allied with God in the eventual salvation of the world and that Satan's enmity is the cause of woman's suffering.[34] Bushnell believes this new woman in Christ to be the mother of the seed—which is Jesus and also the Church as the mystical body of Christ—and that this new woman in

---

30. Ronning, "The Curse on the Serpent," 326-27.

31. Ibid., 374.

32. Ronning, *The Jewish Targums*, 99.

33. Katharine C. Bushnell, *God's Word to Women: One Hundred Bible Studies on Woman's Place in the Church and Home* (1921; repr., Minneapolis: Christians for Biblical Equality, 2003), 189.

34. Bushnell, *God's Word to Women*, 33.

Christ would lead humans out of egotism into the liberty of God's children.[35] Woman is not only the progenitor of the coming destroyer of Satan and his power but also, in her own person, Satan's enemy.[36] Bushnell sees this last point as very important and imagines that Satan would wish to cripple her and, through her husband, hamper her activities so that she could not contend with Satan successfully.[37] To Bushnell, the "enmity" between woman and Satan was that the woman would no longer be associated with God's great enemy.[38] Bushnell believes that there are problems in the world that God has only called women to solve, the answers to which are found in the truths of the Word of God.[39] Bushnell, therefore, views Gen 3:15 as a great promise to both women and humanity in general, yet she does not correlate this verse with the Cross in any specific way.

Joseph Ratzinger in his introductory essay on the encyclical *Redemptoris Mater* discusses several issues pertaining to the interpretation of Gen 3:15 in the Bible.[40] First, he sees that theological exegesis looks at a part in terms of the whole and to learn not what once *was* but what is currently *true*.[41] The encyclical also realizes that along with the patriarchal storyline of the

---

35. This is based upon her exegesis of Jer 31:22. Bushnell, *God's Word to Women*, 190.

36. Ibid., 43.

37. Ibid., 43-44.

38. Ibid., 44.

39. Ibid., 6.

40. Joseph Ratzinger, "The Sign of the Woman: An Introductory Essay on the Encyclical *Redemptoris Mater*," in *Mary, the Church at the Source*, J. Ratzinger and H.U. von Balthasar (San Francisco: Ignatius Press, 2005), 1-11, accessed November 17, 2017, http://www.laici.va/content/dam/laici/documenti/donna/teologia/english/the-sign-of-the-woman-introductory-essay-on-the-encyclical-redemptoris-mater.pdf.

41. Ratzinger, "The Sign of the Woman," 2.

Bible, there is a concurrent line in the Old Testament through the matriarchs to Deborah, Esther, Ruth, and *Sophia*.[42] Ratzinger believes that it is important to spot this feminine line and its salvific content and to see that Christologies can include the feminine.[43] Anthropological truth and the truth about God cannot be properly seen without these facts. Likewise, the promise of Gen 3:15 is *to* and *through* the woman.[44] Exegeting Jn 19:27, the encyclical recognizes a personal relationship between every disciple and Mary's feminine and maternal reality that "brings about Christ's taking form in man."[45] This text also relates back to Gen 3:15 by alluding to Mary as "woman," as does the Cana narrative in John. However, along with their Mariology, Pope John Paul II and Ratzinger wrongly view the woman primarily by her motherly task in the battle against evil and as a sign of hope, and they do not make any association between their analysis and Jael or the Cross.

A fourth-century bishop and doctor of the Church, Ambrose, in commenting on the Deborah, Barak, and the Jael story states, "And so according to this history a woman, that the minds of women might be stirred up, became a judge, a woman set all in order, a woman prophesied, a woman triumphed, and joining in the battle array taught men to war under a woman's lead. But in a mystery it is the battle of faith and the victory of the church" (*Concerning Widows* 8.47-50).[46] Thus, Ambrose recognizes Deborah's leadership and her skill in teaching her army how

---

42. Ibid., 4.

43. Ibid., 4.

44. Ibid., 7.

45. Ibid., 9.

46. J. R. Franke, ed., *Old Testament IV: Joshua, Judges, Ruth, 1–2 Samuel* (Downers Grove, IL: InterVarsity Press, 2005), 117.

to follow her, and believes that this happened so that women might be encouraged. Yet, rather than actual human foes, Deborah and Jael's battle is likened to the battle Christians wage in the realm of faith and the victory the Church enjoys.

The third-century Church father Origen also sees Jael as the Church, using the power of the Cross to fight carnal vices and selfish delights:

> What, therefore, does the web of all this mystical history show us? The woman Jael, that foreigner about whom Deborah's prophecy said that victory would be had "through the hand of a woman," symbolizes the church, which was assembled from foreign nations. . . . (Jael) killed (Sisera) with a stake, then, which is to say that she overthrew him by the power and cunning of the wood of the cross (*Homilies on Judges* 5.5).[47]

With Ambrose, Origen likens Jael to the Church, but most interesting to note is that the Cross is matched by Origen with Jael's tent peg. Not only that but Origen also sees 'cunning' in the cross itself.

From this review of the literature surrounding the idea of a narrative pattern allusion underlying the Gospels' crucifixion and resurrection accounts, some of the most important conclusions are: (1) a literary approach reveals that the Old Testament biblical stories transformed with retellings; (2) in the New Testament, authors see plot twists with the coming of Jesus Christ; (3) the possibility of a narrative pattern is strengthened with multiple allusions and a general following of the marked text's sequence of events; (4) the purpose of the use of fulfillment narrative patterns—beyond the actual prophetic fulfillment

---

47. Franke, *Old Testament IV*, 117.

of the prefiguration story—is often to lead the reader into the comparison of the two stories and to inspire their agency; (5) quotes, allusions, echoes, and narrative patterns can overlay one another; (6) narrative material, when alluded to in the New Testament, doesn't typically use citation formulas or direct quotations; (7) historically, very few people have made much of Jael as a deliverer, even in the arts; (8) theologically, even fewer have pointed to a feminine storyline running through the Old Testament; (9) however, Hamilton and Ronning have shown that the Gen 3:15 promise does run as a thread through Scripture, often in literalistic ways such as in the story of Jael; and (10) Calderón, Ronning, and Origen tie Jael's actions to the Cross.

Some Key Terms

Outside of biblical studies, the definition of the term *intertextuality* revolves around inherited cultural knowledge and relations among texts. Within biblical studies the term *inner-biblical allusion* is often used for a quote, allusion, echo or narrative pattern. However in this project, *intertextuality* will refer to what are termed *inner-biblical allusions* elsewhere to be able to further distinguish the several types of allusions that the biblical texts contain and so as not to be confused with the more narrow term *allusion* itself.

The expression *Jael story*, as used within this project, shall refer to both the narrative of the events involving Jael in Judg 4 as well as Deborah's Song in Judg 5. Jeannine Brown claims a "reader experiences (a) reference to Abraham (for instance) as a storied reference not necessarily tied or limited to a specific Old

Testament text."[48] Therefore, when the audience of the crucifixion and resurrection narratives heard the correspondence, their personal recall of the Jael story would include not just the Judg 4 narrative material but also the Song of Deborah, too.

A *narrative pattern*, as defined by Peter Mallen, is "a series of events or interactions between characters whose similarity to those in an earlier text is apparent although the specific details and the language of expression may vary."[49]

A *fulfillment narrative pattern*, as used in this study, will refer to an Old Testament prophecy or any narrative pattern in general that comes to its fulfillment in Jesus Christ.

The *crucifixion and resurrection narrative accounts* referred to in this study will only be speaking of the passages of Matt 27:33-28:15, Mk 15:22-16:6, Luke 23:33-24:8, and John 19:17-20:5, unless noted otherwise. The reason these passages are chosen is because these contain the elements that specifically correspond to the Jael story.

A *literalistic fulfillment* is a term used by John Ronning to explain the connection between the promise in Gen 3:15 of the offspring of the woman crushing the Serpent's head and Jael's actual crushing of Sisera's head. Ronning states, "I refer to these as 'literalistic' fulfillments because there is an aspect to the event which recalls the literal picture of a man striking a snake on its head given by Gen 3:15. At the same time, it is not a completely literal picture, since we are dealing with humans, not literal snakes."[50] Even though it is not completely literal, Sisera is referred to in this book as a "serpent-figure," since, as

---

48. Brown, "Metalepsis," 32.

49. Mallen, *Isaiah in Luke-Acts*, 24.

50 Ronning, "The Curse on the Serpent," 292.

an enemy of God, he carries on the attack against God's people begun in Genesis 3.

Moreover, this study shall posit that the *offspring of the woman* is "God's new creation," as John Ronning suggests.[51] However in this study the "offspring of the woman" will be more precisely said to be a *representative* of God's new creation.

Structure

The roadmap of this book is as follows. Chapter 1 argues that the Gospel writers, following Jesus himself, saw the crucifixion and resurrection as the fulfillment of the prophetic sign act of Jael, foreseen and prophesied by the prophet Deborah. Twelve of the elements of concurrence will be looked at individually. Chapter 2 will argue that the warrant for this assertion is because Jael's story elaborates on Gen 3:15 and even reverses the fall narrative of Gen 3. Hence, correspondences between Gen 3:15 and Judg 4 and 5 will be discussed, as well as other places in the Old Testament that further develop this theme such as Zech 10:4. The Conclusion will summarize the arguments supporting the book's thesis, suggest what effect the fusion inherent in the metalepsis creates—which includes application for today—and posit areas for further theological research into this topic.

---

51. John Ronning, "Seven Keys to the Interpretation of Genesis 3:15," (recording of lecture at Evangelical Theological Society's Eastern Region meeting, April 6-7, 2018), accessed July 28, 2018, http://www.wordmp3.com/details.aspx?id=27929.

ONE

THE JAEL STORY, GOLGOTHA
AND THE EMPTY TOMB

(Jael) killed (Sisera) with a stake, then, which is to say that she
overthrew him by the power and cunning of the wood of the cross.
—Origen, *Homilies on Judges* 5.5.[52]

Given the replication of the seemingly insignificant details
within each of the Gospel narratives of the crucifixion and resurrection—the place name, the drink, the divided clothes, the
early dawn, and the looking inside the tomb—these details seem
to be important. Likewise, it would be odd if the Gospel writers,
who made great use of quotes, allusions, and echoes to the Old
Testament in their writings to explicate and show the fulfillment
of God's promises in Jesus, did not also see a broad intertextual

52. Franke, *Old Testament IV*, 117.

narrative pattern explaining these minute details. In fact, when Jesus appeared to the disciples on the road to Emmaus, he said he could be found in *all* of the Scriptures and *all* of the prophets (Luke 24:25-27, also Matt 5:17, Luke 24: 25-27, John 5:39). New Testament scholars "read backwards" and often see Christ foreshadowed and acting through Moses,[53] King David,[54] etc. Few, however, see him foreshadowed in any female characters' actions. This study claims, though, that Christ's death and resurrection is foreshadowed in the New Testament by Jael's story within the Gospels, providing a clear articulation of the reasons for the Cross and Resurrection. Focusing on the trees of quotes, allusions, and echoes, scholars have missed the forest of this broader narrative pattern.

Like Jesus' crucifixion itself, the story of Jael's action is a violent and gruesome spectacle, but this was necessary in both cases for God to bring his deliverance. The story of Jael—using just the elements that are alluded to in the Gospels' accounts—goes as follows (the common narrative elements are italicized): King Jabin's general, Sisera, was fleeing from the battle that his army had just lost against Israel. Marching out against King Jabin's army, which resulted in the *earth quaking* before him,

---

53. For instance, "The account of Jesus' transfiguration on the mountain in Matthew 17 is a transformation of Moses' revelation on Sinai in Exodus 24.6 The basic elements remain the same—a trip up the mountain, God speaking from a cloud, seven days, changes in appearance, etc. But these elements have been transferred to a new context." Gil Rosenberg, "Hypertextuality," in *Exploring Intertextuality: Diverse Strategies for New Testament Interpretation of Texts*, ed. B. J. Oropeza and Steve Moyise (Eugene, OR: Cascade Books, 2016), 18.

54. Scot McKnight mentions that Jesus is from the house of David in Luke and that when "Matthew organizes Israel's history into three groups of fourteen, he is showing that all of Israel's Story has a Davidic shape, and that Davidic Story comes to completion in the complete Davidic King, Jesus, son of Mary and Joseph, Messiah of Israel." Scot McKnight, *The King Jesus Gospel: The Original Good News Revisited* (Grand Rapids, MI: Zondervan, 2011), 86-94.

God had acted as a divine warrior against King Jabin, subduing him. General Sisera sought refuge with Jael. Sisera said to her, "*I am thirsty.*" She gave him *a drink.* Sisera commanded her to *stand guard at the entrance* of the tent and *say to anyone who comes* and asks if a man is here, "*There is not.*" Jael disobeyed him, though. She took a tent peg nail and hammered Sisera, striking and piercing his skull so that the peg went into the ground. In the meantime, Sisera's mother was wondering about Sisera's absence, so her ladies said to her, "Are they not *dividing up the spoil*—one girl *for each soldier* and also *the clothes*?" After Jael struck Sisera's head, he lost consciousness, *was darkened,* and died. Barak, the Israelite general, *came looking* for Sisera, and standing *outside of the tent-tomb* Jael said to him, "*Come here and I will show you the man whom you are seeking.*" Barak went into the tent and saw Sisera's *corpse.* The prophet Deborah said, "So perish all your enemies, O Lord! But may *your friends who love you be like the sun as it rises in its power.*" After this, Israel was *undisturbed for 40 years.*

Using just the specific texts that match the Jael story, the combined Gospels' account of the crucifixion and resurrection of Jesus results in a very similar story (common narrative elements again italicized): Jesus was brought to the place of *a skull.* On the cross he said, "*I am thirsty,*" and they offered him *a drink.* They crucified him and *divided up his clothes amongst themselves, one part for each* soldier. When Jesus died, the *earth was quaking* and *darkness came over* the whole land. At the chief priests' and the Pharisees' request, Pilate commanded that soldiers should *stand guard outside the tomb.* On the first day of the week, *when the sun was rising,* the women went to the tomb. The angels *outside the tomb* said to them, "*He is not here,* but has risen" and "*Come see the place where he lay.*" When they went in, they did not find *a corpse,* however. After this, Jerusalem *was undisturbed for* (around) *40 years* until its destruction in AD 70.

It is important to point out that not only are there at least ten obvious points of concurrence, but these narrative elements follow basically the same order. These elements can also be seen to be fulfilling the Old Testament biblical type-scene of a woman crushing the head of a serpent-figure, as the offspring of the woman does in Gen 3:15. Such type-scenes are illuminated by recurring words and short phrases, or they can be seen in actions, a sequence of actions or ideas replayed.[55] Robert Alter notes, "The type-scene is not merely a way of formally recognizing a particular kind of narrative moment; it is also a means of attaching that moment to a larger pattern of historical and theological meaning."[56] Therefore, the crucifixion and resurrection narratives' intertextuality with the Jael story functions to show the audience how Jesus is not defeated in his crucifixion but is fulfilling God's ancient covenant promise in the *protoevangelium* by actually crushing the fountainhead of the Serpent. The table that follows looks more closely at twelve correspondences between the Old Testament Jael story and the Gospels' crucifixion and resurrection accounts. After this, these narrative elements will be discussed each in turn.

---

55. Robert Alter, *The Art of the Biblical Narrative* (Basic Books, 1981), 95.
56. Alter, *Art of Biblical Narrative*, 60.

TABLE ON GOSPELS' CHRONOLOGICAL INTERTEXTUALITY WITH JUDGES[B] 4/5

NETS for Judges and NRSV for segments of verses in the Gospels, unless noted

Chronological Gospel Crucifixion/ Resurrection Accounts (NRSV)	Judges 4 (NETS, unless noted)	Judges 5 (NETS, unless noted)	Comments
Place of the Skull/ Golgotha Mt 27:33 called Golgotha (which means place of a skull) Mk 15:22 called Golgotha (which means place of a skull) Lk 23:33 called The Skull Jn 19:17 called the Place of the Skull, which in Hebrew is called Golgotha	**4:21** drove the peg in his temple, and it went through in the ground	**5:26b** She put her left hand to a peg, and her right hand to a hammer of laborers, and she hammered Sisara; she pierced his head, and she struck; she pierced his temple.	This verse serves as a reference *marker* for the section in the Gospels back to Judg 4/5 and also Judg 9, a doublet of the Jael story. In Judg 9:53 ("But a certain woman threw an upper millstone on Abimelech's head, and crushed his skull." NRSV), *skull* is *gulgoleth* in Hebrew.
Drink Mt 27:34 they offered him wine to drink … he would not drink it Mk 15:23 they offered him wine … he did not take it (Also, Mk 15:36) Jn 19:28 he said, in order to fulfill Scripture, "I am thirsty."	**4:19** And Sisara said to her, "Do but give me a little water to drink, for I am thirsty." She opened the skin of milk and gave him a drink	**5:25** He asked for water; she gave him milk	Luke does not include this event, and John has the drink placed later in his sequence.

Chronological Gospel Accounts	Judges 4	Judges 5	Comments
When crucified Mt 27:35 and when they had crucified him Mk 15:22 And they crucified him Lk 23:33 they crucified him Jn 19:18 There they crucified him	**4:21** drove the peg in his temple, and it went through in the ground	**5:26** She put her left hand to a peg, and her right hand to a hammer of laborers, and she hammered Sisara; she pierced his head, and she struck; she pierced his temple.	
Divided Clothes Mt 27:35 they divided his clothes among themselves Mk 15:24 divided his clothes among them Lk 23:33 to divide his clothing Jn 19:23-25 took his clothes and divided them into four parts, one for each soldier		**5:30** "Are they not finding and dividing the spoil?—A girl or two for every man; spoil of dyed stuffs for Sisera, spoil of dyed stuffs embroidered, two pieces of dyed work embroidered for my neck as spoil?" (NRSV)	Lk 23:27-31 should also be considered as a reference to Judg 5:28-30, though it comes before the Golgotha sequences.
Jn only: Pierced Jn 19:37 Another passage of Scripture says, "They will look on the one whom they have pierced."			Only John has the reference to "pierced," which may allude to the doublet Judg 9:54b (So the young man pierced him through, and he died, NASB). *Pierced* is ἐκκεντέω in both.

Chronological Gospel Accounts	Judges 4	Judges 5	Comments
Mt only: Earthquakes Mt 27:51 At that moment the curtain of the temple was torn in two, from top to bottom. The earth shook (σείω), and the rocks were split	**Possibly an indirect reference in 4:23** And in that day God routed King Iabin of Chanaan before the sons of Israel.	**(5:4, 5)** "Lord, at your marching out in Seir, when you set out from the field of Edom, earth trembled (σείω), and the sky dripped dews, and the clouds dripped water. Mountains quaked (σείω) from before the lord Eloi"	Note the earthquake references are earlier in the Judg 5 sequence, though. [Also, Mt 27:54 saw the earthquake (σεισμός) and Mt 28:2 mentions a great earthquake (σεισμός).]
Darkness came over Mt 27:45 darkness (σκότος) came over the whole land Mk 15:33 darkness (σκότος) came over the whole land Lk 23:44,45 darkness (σκότος) came over the whole land, ... sun's light failed, and the curtain was torn in two	**4:21b** (Sisera) becoming confused (or having lost consciousness he) was darkened (σκοτόω), and died. [LXX^B, Trent C. Butler, *Judges, Volume 8* (Grand Rapids, MI: Zondervan, 2009), 81n21.e.]		John does not include the darkness event.
Mt only: Guard the tomb Mt 27:64, 65 Command the tomb to be made secure ... You have a guard of soldiers, go make it as secure as you can	**(4:20)** And he said to her, "Do stand at the entrance of the tent"		Note that the reference to Judg 4:20 is earlier in the Judg 4 sequence, though.

Chronological Gospel Accounts	Judges 4	Judges 5	Comments
Dawning sun, they went Mt 28:1 as the first day of the week was dawning, Mary Magdalene and the other Mary went Mk 16:2 And very early on the first day of the week, when the sun had risen, they went Lk 24:1 at early dawn, they came to the tomb Jn 20:1 while it was still dark, Mary Magdalene came to the tomb		**5:31a** "So perish all your enemies, O Lord! And may those who love him be like the marching out of the sun in its power." "So perish all your enemies, O LORD! But may your friends be like the sun as it rises in its might." (NRSV)	
Mt, Mk, Lk: He is not here Mt 28:6 he is not here Mt 28:12 After the priests had assembled with the elders, … telling them, "You must say, 'His disciples came by night and stole him away while we were asleep.'" Mk 16:6 he is not here Lk 24:6 he is not here	**(4:20)** "if a man comes to you and asks you and says, 'Is there a man here?' that you will say, 'There is not.'" ('ên, lit., "nothing, no-one").		

Chronological Gospel Accounts	Judges 4	Judges 5	Comments
Come see the place Mt 28:5 "Come see the place where he lay" Mk 16:6 Look, there is the place they laid him Lk 24:3 but when they went in, they did not find the body…"Why do you look for the living among the dead? He is not here, but has risen" (Jn 20:15 Jesus said to her, "Woman, why are you weeping? Whom are you looking for …")	**4:22** and Jael went out to meet him and said to him, "Come here, and I will show you the man whom you are seeking." And he went in to her, and see, Sisara sprawled, a corpse, and the tent peg in his temple.		Note that this event in John comes before the dawning sun/they went scene, whereas the Synoptics have it before it.
		5:31b And the land was undisturbed for forty years (NASB).	It is around forty years after the resurrection that Jerusalem is destroyed in AD 70 in prophetic fulfillment of the prophet Deborah's Song.

Analysis of Concurring Texts

Place of the Skull/Golgotha, Matt 27:33, Mk 15:22, Luke 23:33, Jn 19:17, Judg 4:21, 5:26, 9:53. Recalling Ziva Ben-Porat's ideas on markers, the mention of Golgotha and "The Place of a Skull" can be thought of as a marker and an immediate indication for a Jewish audience—and even for some of the Gentile audiences—that the author is about to tell a story in which someone's head gets crushed. Except for Luke, the Gospels each mention this place name in two ways. A knowledgeable audience would specifically hear a reference to the doublet of the Jael story in Judg 9 where a woman drops a millstone from a tower and crushes the skull—the golgotha—of the enemy general Abimelech.[57] James Hamilton says, "Bad guys get broken heads in the Bible,"[58] yet the Hebrew term gulĕggōlet (skull) is only used in Judg 9:53 as a skull that is broken, so the audience could hear specifically a reference to the Judg 9 Jael doublet story.[59] These two stories share borrowed vocabulary and imagery, yet the audience would not know which text, if any, was being alluded to: they would just recall the thematic image and concept. To establish intertextuality between the texts the same actual vocabulary is not as important as the imagery, as Thomas Schreiner elaborates.[60]

---

57. Hamilton states, "The term gulĕggōlet (skull) is used to describe the crushing of Abimelech's head in Judg 9:53. This term appears to have been transliterated (perhaps via Aramaic) into Greek as Golgotha (cf. BDAG, 204), which is transliterated into English as Golgotha." Hamilton, "The Skull Crushing Seed of the Woman," 53n89.

58. Ibid., 34.

59. See also the section below titled "When crucified" for the reason an audience might hear an allusion to the Jael story.

60. See other examples of thematic imagery allusions to Gen 3:15 in Thomas R. Schreiner, "Foundations for Faith," *The Southern Baptist Journal of Theology*

Cynthia Edenburg notes that a doublet of "parallel accounts may function as a poetic device for depicting recurring events or may serve to preset a common theme from different viewpoints,"[61] and that "doublets awaken within the reader a sense of *déjà vu*, which spurs him to examine the relationship between the stories in order to determine whether they are recurring accounts of the single event, or rather similar accounts of distinctive events."[62] The author of Judges here seems to be pointing to recurring events with the common theme of how God is beginning to fulfill his promise to his people to crush the head of their enemy through the seed of the woman (as will be further discussed in Chapter 2). Furthermore, repetition is a key feature in Old Testament writings to draw attention to something.[63] Robert Alter states that "the two most distinctively (OT) biblical uses of repeated action are when we are given two versions of the same event and when the same event, with minor variations, occurs at different junctures of the narrative, usually involving different characters or sets of characters, . . . (sometimes) setting two occurrences of the same type-scene in close sequence" (parentheticals added).[64] This appears to be the case with the Judges' Jael story and the woman who drops

---

(September 2001): 2-3, accessed July 21, 2018, http://resources.thegospelcoalition.org/library/editorial-foundations-for-faith.

61. Cynthia Edenburg, "How (Not) to Murder a King: Variations on a Theme in 1 Sam 24; 26." *Scandinavian Journal of the Old Testament* 12, no.1 (1998): 67.

62. Edenburg, "How (Not) to Murder a King," 66.

63. A word-motif in the repetition of certain key-words, "as a good many commentators have recognized, is one of the most common features of the narrative art of the (Hebrew) Bible. But in biblical prose, the reiteration of key-words has been formalized into a prominent convention which is made to play a much more central role in the development of thematic argument than does the repetition of such key-words in other narrative traditions" (parenthetical added). Alter, *The Art of the Biblical Narrative*, 92.

64. Alter, *The Art of the Biblical Narrative*, 181.

the millstone on Abimelech's *gulgoleth* or skull. Even as late as the Qumran community, there was a practice of connecting texts by themes, ideas or catchwords,[65] so it is reasonable to assume that such a double mention of Golgotha and Skull would serve as a marker for those in the New Testament times' audience.

Drink, Mt 27:34, Mk 15:23, 36; Jn 19:28, Judg 4:19, 5:25. All but Luke include this event, yet in John the focus is instead upon Jesus drinking it and not trying and refusing it as he does in the Synoptics, and that Jesus' request is actually in fulfillment of Scripture. Which scripture, though? While the Greek phrase which the Gospel of John uses to say "I am thirsty" is not verbatim from the Septuagint texts of Sisera's "I am thirsty" (Judg 4:19), it is very close.[66] Ben Witherington notes that commentators have long debated on the source of the "I am thirsty" citation in John 19:28, with Ps 69:21 being assumed by most.[67]

Since Matthew's formula quotations are all from the Prophets, an allusion in Matt 27:34 to the Former Prophet Book of Judges and a saying of the prophet Deborah would be in keeping with Matthew's allusions to the Prophets.[68] This idea is supported by Daniel Block in *The New American Commentary* series when he says, "Although the Song makes no direct reference to her prophetic involvement, it arises out of Deborah's prophetic self-consciousness. By placing the ode in Deborah's mouth, the

---

65. A single papyrus "included four paragraphs with quotations from Deuteronomy 5:28-29 and 18:18-19; Numbers 24:15-17; Deuteronomy 33: 8-11; and Apocryphon of Joshua … Short phrases or sentences introduce each of these four citations." Witherington, *Torah Old and New*, 9.

66. All scriptures included will be from the NRSV, unless otherwise noted.

67. Witherington, *Torah Old and New*, 6.

68. See another instance of this in the divided clothes event mentioned below.

author of the book correctly recognizes that **her interpretation of the battle is fundamentally a prophetic word**" (emphasis added).[69] That is, the Song of Deborah is not just another Old Testament narrative—since it is sung by the prophet Deborah herself, it is considered a prophetic description. In this sense she is like Miriam before her and most of the prophets after her who also speak in poetry.[70]

So is it possible that Jesus' "I am thirsty" saying in Jn 19:28 is a reference to both Ps 69:21 and Judg 4:19? According to John McHugh, M. André Feuillet believes the Fourth Gospel writer is, in general, following rabbinical precedents by using terms that can refer to both the Pentateuch and the Prophets. He cites the "Behold the Lamb of God" saying in Jn 1:29, 36 as recalling both the Passover Lamb and the Servant of Isaiah, who was led like a lamb to the slaughter. Feuillet also sees the living water in the Gospel of John as recalling both Ex 17:4-7 and Ezek 47:1-2.[71] And as was previously mentioned, John 12:31-33 has three over-laying images that are prefigurations of the crucifixion and res-urrection, including the one from Num 21 with the serpent on a pole. It is not irrational then to assume that there are superim-posed images and double and triple allusions in John's crucifixion and resurrection narratives, as well. The sentence "I am thirsty" could then be a fulfillment of both Ps 69:21 and Judg 4:19.

Interestingly if Jesus saw his upcoming crucifixion as a rep-resentation of the serpent on the pole from Num 21 in John 12:31-31, repeating Sisera's "I am thirsty" would also see Jesus

---

69. D. I. Block, *Judges, Ruth* (Nashville: Broadman & Holman Publishers, 1999), 215.

70. It should be noted here that Hebrew poetry in that time, unlike modern poetry that is mostly based on rhyming words, was based on similar images.

71. John McHugh, *The Mother of Jesus in the New Testament* (London: Darton, Long-man & Todd, 1975), 385.

as taking the place of a serpent-figure. As Ben Witherington points out, "All layers of the Gospel tradition, Mark, Q, special M, special L, and John are in agreement that Jesus on occasion referred the Scriptures *to himself*, or suggested they were being fulfilled in his ministry, his works, and his deeds."[72] If proved, this allusion to Sisera would lead to the idea of the Gospel of John emphasizing Jesus' likeness to Sisera and his becoming accursed for us in his crucifixion.

When crucified, Mt 27:35, Mk 15:22, Lk 23:33, Jn 19:18, Judg 4:21, 5:26. Robert Alter discusses the reasons for the Old Testament's use of repetition: "through abundant repetition, the semantic range of (a) word-root is explored, different forms of the roots are deployed, branching off at times into phonetic relatives (that is, wordplay), synonymity, and antonymity; by virtue of its verbal status, the *Leitwort* refers immediately to meaning and thus to theme as well."[73] Likewise, the *leitwort* of skull-crushing is seen in Deborah's Song in the fact that no less than four ways is Sisera's skull damaged, five if one counts Jael driving the peg into his temple in Judg 4:21. Judges 5:26 reads, "she struck (*hālam*) Sisera; she crushed (*māḥaq* 1x in OT) his head; she shattered (*māḥaṣ*) and pierced (*ḥālap*, only time with this meaning in the OT) his temple (*raqqāh*)."[74] Deborah, through her repetition, is most likely pointing to the thematic significance of God initially fulfilling his promise in Gen 3:15 that the offspring of the woman would crush the head of his enemy. It is also reasonable to imagine that, in the same way, the fact that the Gospels' place name, Golgotha and Place of a Skull, is mentioned in two

---

72. Witherington, *Torah Old and New*, 31.

73. Alter, *The Art of the Biblical Narrative*, 95.

74. Hamilton, "The Skull Crushing Seed of the Woman," 50n50.

different ways mirrors this particular verse with its repetition.

The hammering and nailing imagery involved in the act of crucifixion, too, is a clear echo to Judg 5:26's peg and hammering. It should also be mentioned here that—contrary to many commentators on Jael—Jack Sasson in *The Anchor Yale Bible* makes it obvious that Jael's encounter with Sisera cannot logistically be sexual, given that in Judg 5 they are both standing when she crushes his head and he falls to the ground at her feet in defeat.[75] It also ought to be underscored that Jael's tent peg is noted in the Judg 4 story as being driven "into the ground," just like a cross in a crucifixion, as was recognized previously by Ronning.

J. Clinton McCann in the *Interpretation* series makes a further point about Judg 4 saying,

> From the narrator's point of view, Jael's actions are completely justified. Jael is both expedient and clever, for she recognizes and removes the one who is clearly presented as a threat to her and to her household's honor. Sisera's actions, particularly his second request (asking her to lie), give Jael every reason to believe that her life and her household's are in danger. From the narrator's point of view, Jael's killing is not murder, but rather self-defense. It constitutes also, as suggested above, God's action (4:23) (parenthetical added).[76]

Many modern scholars fault Jael's lack of hospitality, yet the first audience of the Jael story would have recognized the breaking of the rules of hospitality by Sisera instead.[77] Also, Scripture

---

75. Jack M. Sasson, *Judges 1–12* (New Haven: Yale University Press, 2014), 317.

76. J. Clinton McCann, *Judges* (Louisville, KY: Westminster John Knox Press, 2011), 54.

77. McCann, *Judges*, 54.

states it was God acting through Jael to defeat his enemy, the cruel oppressor King Jabin. K. Lawson Younger in *The NIV Application Commentary* notes that in the Jael story "the cycle's satirization of the military commander Sisera as an agent of Jabin's oppressive foreign kingship is in contrast to the glorification of Yahweh, who controls all circumstances that lead to Israel's deliverance—both those of the temporal order in the prose portrayal and those of the cosmic order, with which Jael's actions are consonant, in the hymnic portrayal."[78] God, therefore, subdued King Jabin through Jael. Likewise, God subdued Satan through Jesus in his crucifixion.

Divided Clothes, Mt 27:35, Mk 15:24, Lk 23:27-31, 33; Jn 19:18; Judg 5:28-30. "Aren't they finding, dividing the spoil? A young girl or two for the chief hero, colored cloth as spoil for Sisera?"[79] asks Sisera's mother's lady (Judg 5:30). Rather, Israel was being freed from such an experience at the very same moment. Correspondingly, the Roman soldiers appear to be dividing up the spoils of Jesus' crucifixion by dividing his clothes amongst themselves, yet ironically, it is the spiritual Roman oppression that followers of Jesus will soon be freed from. Rather than Rome's actions then signalling its victory over Jesus, followers of Jesus will be released from Rome's spiritual chains.

Scholars usually see the divided clothes event as prefigured in Ps 22:18—"they divide my clothes among themselves, and for my clothing they cast lots"—yet the Gospels' event can also be seen as a fulfillment of Judg 5:30. Richard Hays recognizes, "It is perhaps noteworthy that all ten authentic Matthean formula

78. K. L. Younger, Jr., *Judges and Ruth* (Grand Rapids, MI: Zondervan, 2002), 158–59.
79. Trent C. Butler, *Judges, Volume 8* (Grand Rapids, MI: Zondervan, 2009), 116.

quotations cite texts from the prophets, whereas the text cited in 27:35 is Ps 22:19, making the formulaic (*to rathen dia tou prophatou*) not strictly appropriate, unless the psalmist should be regarded as a prophet."[80] So although Matt 27:35 doesn't use the formulaic "to fulfill what had been spoken through the prophet," a reference to Judg 5:30 in the Former Prophets Book of Judges from the prophet Deborah would better align with the importance to Matthew of citations from the prophets.

It can be suggested that Luke alludes to this Judg 5 divided clothes event twice: once in the regular order and once beforehand, when Jesus speaks to the "daughters of Jerusalem." In the Judg 5:28-30 passage, Sisera's mother's ladies look out from latticed windows, which could signify their affluence, ease and comfort, especially in contrast to the tent-dwelling Jael. They have status and wealth, perhaps gained from oppressing Israel. Ron Pierce also states:

> This Canaanite woman of privilege calms her anxiety and fears regarding her son's late return by imagining his violent abuse of young Israelite virgins—a common practice in ancient warfare. She exclaims (literally), "A womb or two for every head." She describes them by their reproductive organs (*raham rachamatayim*) as "unspoiled girls" taken among the "spoils." They may be used for instant gratification or kept as conjugal conveniences to produce progeny.[81]

Sisera's mother and her spiritual daughters, her ladies, are incorrectly imagining this happening to the Israelite daughters, yet this may be in their own futures. Correspondingly, Jesus

---

80. Hays, *Echoes of Scripture in the Gospels*, 391n5.

81. Ronald W. Pierce, "Deborah: Troublesome Woman or Woman of Valor?" *Priscilla Papers* 32, no. 2 (Spring 2018): 5-6, accessed June 8, 2018, https://www.cbeinternational.org/sites/default/files/PP322-pierce.pdf.

THE CROSS AND THE TENT PEG

has some lamenting words to say to the daughters of Jerusalem to "weep for yourselves and your children" (Luke 23:27-31), perhaps foreseeing the destruction of Jerusalem in around forty years (Judg 5:31) and the women's and their daughters' plight during it.

Pierced, Jn 19:37, Judg 9:54. "Another passage of scripture says, 'they will look on the one whom they have pierced'" (Jn 19:37). This event is usually considered to be a fulfillment of Zech 12:10. It can also be argued that it is an allusion to the doublet of the Jael story in Judg 9:54b: "Then he called quickly to the young man, his armor bearer, and said to him, 'Draw your sword and kill me, so that it will not be said of me, "A woman slew him."' So the young man pierced him through, and he died" (NASB). Similarly, Jesus' side being pierced and blood and water coming out is what indicates to the soldiers that he is dead. *Pierced* is, likewise, ἐκκεντέω in both texts. Seeing this event as doubly citing the Judg 9 passage would also align with the Gospel of John's possible emphasis upon Jesus *receiving* the drink, as mentioned above, since it would place Jesus on the Cross in a substitutionary role as a sinful Abimelech or Sisera, or as an offspring of the Serpent.

Earthquakes, Mt 27:51, 54; 28:2; Judg 4:23, 5:4, 5. There are two earthquakes in Matt, the first mentioned twice, and all three mentions emphasizing God's delivering action. One happened when the curtain of the temple was torn (27:51); another mention was that the earthquake itself caused the first person, a Roman centurion, to recognize Jesus in his crucifixion as God's son (27:54); and the third was when the angel of the Lord rolled back the stone from the tomb and sat on it. These can rightly be considered a sign that God was opening the way to himself in the Holy of Holies, in revealing Jesus Christ as the second person of the Godhead, and in raising Jesus from the dead.

The Song of Deborah contains earthquakes as signifying the action of God, as well. Concerning Judg 5:4-5, Trent Butler in *Word Biblical Commentary* declares:

> The theophany paints the theological and dramatic backdrop against which all else is to be heard. The poetic focus is on God coming to his people, a people who are freely volunteering themselves to fight God's war. The theophany ties Israel's previous experiences in holy war, particularly experiences in the exodus, to Israel's present situation. The God of the exodus is still the God who comes to help his dedicated people. Thus, the theophany also establishes reason to praise Yahweh from the beginning, even before the battle results are reported.[82]

The people are to sing of God's praises in hope and faith in his coming delivering actions; Yahweh brings deliverance for his people who co-labor with him. This is true of the new deliverance that begins in the Resurrection as well, when the way to God is released, people's eyes are opened to see God in the Son, and resurrection life in Jesus begins, corresponding to each of the Gospel of Matthew's mentions of earthquakes.

Noting that the exodus is portrayed as a renewal of creation, J. Clinton McCann concludes, "In short, the theophany in Judg 4:4-5 reinforces the conclusion that God is behind all the action behind Chapters 4-5, and that it all has ultimately to do with the establishment of life as God intends it."[83] The apocalyptic

---

82. Butler, *Judges*, 166.
83. McCann, *Judges*, 60.

character of the earthquakes in Matt also indicates that God is establishing new creation and that worship and thanksgiving from his people is the proper response.

Darkness came over, Mt 27:45, Mk 15:33, Lk 23:44, 45; Judg 4:21. "(Sisera) becoming confused (or having lost consciousness he) was darkened (σκοτόω) and died" (Judg 4:21).[84] The triple tradition notes, correspondingly, that darkness came over the whole land when Jesus died. This is another sign—like the earthquakes—that God was acting, yet it has a slightly different connotation. All three of the Gospel passages utilize the same root of the word "darkness" (σκότος). BDAG has this word literally meaning "of the darkness in the depths of the sea" and sees the darkness in these Synoptic accounts as "the darkness of chaos," echoing Gen 1:2's darkness (cf. Mt 8:12, Mt 22:13, Mt 25:30). BDAG includes three more definitions, namely, 1) "the state of being unknown," such as things that are hidden in darkness (1 Cor 4:5); 2) "the state of spiritual or moral darkness" because of being darkened by sin, which is also "the state of unbelievers and of the godless" (Mt 4:16, 6:23b; Luke 1:79, 22:53; Jn 3:19; and 3) "the bearer/victim/instrument of darkness" (Mt 6:23a; Lk 11:35; Eph 5:8).[85] "Darkness and chaos reign, and if the light in you is darkness, how great is that darkness!" (Matt 6:23b, cf. Luke 22:53). Each of these definitions in the Synoptics' crucifixion and resurrection accounts can apply to the imagery of the darkness of the world. As Sisera was darkened and died, it can be suggested that he and his skull, paralleled in the Synoptics, represent all

---

84. Butler, *Judges*, 81n21.e.

85. W. Arndt et al., *A Greek-English Lexicon of the New Testament and Other Early Christian Literature*, 3rd ed. (Chicago: University of Chicago Press, 2000), 932.

of the world under the reign of chaos, evil, and moral and spiritual darkness. As Origen sees it, Jael overthrew Sisera by the power and cunning of the wood of the cross;" analogously, God overpowers the Prince of Darkness with the power of the cross (Judg 4:23).

Guard the tomb, Mt 27:64-65, Judg 4:20. General Sisera was used to giving commands and so told Jael, "Stand at the entrance of the tent, and if anybody comes and asks you, 'Is anyone here?' say, 'No.'" (Judg 4:20). Similarly, the chief priests and Pharisees pushed Pilate saying, "Command the tomb to be made secure," so that no one would steal Jesus' body, so Pilate gave the command. The lie that Sisera wanted Jael to tell also foreshadows when the chief priests and elders in Matt 28:12 "devised a plan to give a large sum of money to the soldiers, telling them, 'You must say, "His disciples came by night and stole him away while we were asleep."'" The imagery is quite congruent.

Dawning sun, they went, Mt 28:1, Mk 16:2, Lk 24:1, Jn 20:1, Judg 5:31. "May those who love him be like the mighty sun as it rises" (Judg 5:31).[86] Ronning notes, "Judges 5:31 (where the wording is similar to *Tos. Tg. Zech.* 2:10) speaks of the sun going forth in its strength as a simile for the righteous, in contrast to the LORD's enemies, who perish."[87] This verse is echoed very clearly in the imagery of the quadruple tradition of the righteous women going forth at the break of dawn. It should be noted that all four Gospel writers also keep the two ideas of the women going forth and the breaking dawn within the same sentence—stressing the intertextuality.

---

86. Butler, *Judges*, 116.
87. Ronning, *The Jewish Targums*, 28.

The curse and blessing of Judg 5:31 highlights the contrast between God's enemies and the righteous. "(Jael's) willingness to risk her life is in greatly heightened contrast to the Israelite tribes who choose to remain at home, to play it safe," says Younger.[88] "As the final verse of the poem (5:31) suggests, Jael, along with Deborah and Barak, is among God's friends. This final verse implicitly invites contemporary readers to consider how we too may join God in the divine work of crushing oppressors, God's enemies, and so take our place as well among God's friends," posits McCann.[89] Yet, this idea is incorrect, as none of the Gospels have a curse upon "God's enemies" before these sentences. Hays declares, "In some cases, the intertextual links between Scripture and Gospel enact ironic reversals: they require readers to mark the distance traveled between (say) Elijah and Jesus, to recognize the reversal of scriptural topoi. Jesus will raise the dead son of a widow but he will not call down fire from heaven to incinerate his opponents."[90] There is also an ironic reversal with the resurrection—there is no curse corresponding to this implied blessing upon the women advancing to the tomb since God's *true* enemy in the Gospels' crucifixion and resurrection accounts is identified not as people or even spiritual "enemies" but as Satan himself.

He is not here, come see the place, Mt 28:5-6, 12; Mk 16:6; Lk 24:3, 6; Jn 20:15; Judg 4:20, 22. These events indicate the point at which the audience would have recognized a plot twist in the fulfillment narrative pattern of the Jael story. Whereas when Barak looked inside Jael's tent-tomb, he saw a dead Sisera,

---

88. Younger, Jr., *Judges and Ruth*, 161.

89. McCann, *Judges*, 61.

90. Hays, *Echoes of Scripture in the Gospels*, 276.

those who looked inside Jesus' tomb at the angel's suggestion expected Jesus' corpse following the Jael storyline, but, instead, saw no-one. Ironically, this result is exactly what Sisera himself commands Jael to tell those who come looking for him: "'Is there a man here?' that you will say, 'There is nothing'!" This type of plot twist in a biblical type-scene would have been familiar to those versed in the Old Testament narratives, though; Robert Alter states that the Old Testament biblical type-scenes sometimes have "ingenious variations."[91] This plot twist of the empty tomb and the angels' declaration that "he is risen" in the Synoptics indicate the climax of history and the great reversal in the world and the surprising pivot that happened with the resurrection of Jesus Christ. Again, the foreshadowing Jael story assists those hearing the crucifixion and resurrection accounts to understand these events as a fulfillment of God's grand plan of redemption that began in the *protoevangelium* of Gen 3:15 by "attaching (the) moment to a larger pattern of historical and theological meaning."[92] The fulfillment narrative pattern reveals God's trustworthiness.

Forty years, Judg 5:31. In contrast to John Ronning, who views the sun going forth in its strength as a simile for the righteous, Ron Pierce believes the sun to reference God's judgment in Judg 5:31:

> The final reference to the "sun when it goes out in its strength" (a symbol of divine judgment across Scripture, e.g., Jer 4:23) also contains poetic irony as a symbol of Israel's leaders: Deborah a woman of "fire/light," and Barak

---

91. Alter, *The Art of the Biblical Narrative*, 181.
92. Ibid., 60.

a man of "lightning." Because of God's remarkable work through them—as well as through the unlikely Kenite Jael—Israel "has peace for forty years." This single line of prose at the end of the battle hymn speaks to the positive result of, and blessing on, their obedience.[93]

Peace connotes flourishing, though, and the NASB translates this word as "undisturbed," which aligns with both the Hebrew and the LXX texts. The idea of the imagery of the sun indicating *both* the righteous ones as well as judgment from God needs to be further considered, though. Judgment upon Israel versus blessing upon those who volunteer on God's side can be thought to be two sides of this same "sun" coin.

Concerning the theme of judgment in the Book of Judges, Jacob L. Wright argues:

> So one of the fascinating things about the Book of Judges is that it gives a lot of attention to men and women, men, their masculinity, Samson, think of Samson, but also Gideon and Avi hu melekh [Gideon's son]. But it begins with a woman as a judge and after this woman's reign as judge, her period of ruling, everything goes downward. **And when we look through the whole Book of Judges, the downward spiral is mapped out on how these guys, how Israel actually treats their women.** Women are strong at the beginning and then they become the objects of violence at the end; and so they use women to show that in great periods of time, women were treated well, but also governed, were leaders of society and at the end, it goes down toward the masculinity, the typical chauvinistic type of attitude emerges and that goes hand

---

93. Pierce, "Deborah," 6.

in hand with an abuse of women. And when the biblical authors imagined how could Israelite society be depicted in a bad way, they show women being abused (emphasis added).[94]

If we accept that one of the Book of Judges' moral standard is how a people treats women, Israel in the Deborah/Jael story is exemplary in this regard. This idea is also proved with the contrasting character, Abimelech, in Judg 9's, who notably says to his armorbearer, "Draw your sword and kill me, so people will not say about me, 'A woman killed him.'" (Judg 9:54).

This is not a far-fetched conclusion, considering the great importance of *dialogue* in the Old Testament biblical narrative. Robert Alter notes, "Everything in the world of biblical narrative ultimately gravitates toward dialogue;" the declaration of the narrators' views are given their full significance in dialogue, and a character reveals himself most thoroughly in his speech.[95] Therefore it is Abimelech's chauvinism that is being emphasized with what he says to his armorbearer, and it differentiates him from Barak who follows Deborah's leadership and Jael as a (female) deliverer of Israel.

John Goldingay states, "As someone who combined the role of judge, prophet, leader, and poet, there is no doubt that (Deborah) is the greatest figure in the book. It is certainly striking that the only person in Scripture who combines all these roles is a woman."[96] However Butler goes further and notably asks:

---

94. Jacob L. Wright, "What Gender Issues Are Present in the Book of Judges?" Bible Odyssey, accessed July 3, 2018, https://www.bibleodyssey.org/tools/video-gallery/g/gender-issues-judges-wright.

95. Alter, *The Art of Biblical Narrative*, 182.

96. John Goldingay, "Motherhood, Machismo, and the Purpose of Yahweh in Judges 4-5," *Anvil* 12, no. 1 (1995): 24.

Every judge died except for the judge featured in Chaps. 4 and 5. What explains this pregnant omission of the central fact that ties all the other Judges narratives together? . . . With the strong emphasis in both prose and poetry on the role of **Jael as ultimate human deliverer** here, could it be that the editor intentionally makes this narrative the featured piece in his narrative of the judges? Can it be that the volunteerism of the poetry and the individual heroism of the rank outsider in the prose narrative served as the true ideal for the editor? Is this story a true counterpart to Joshua, the perfect leader after Moses though he was not a priest, not a prophet, not a king, not a judge? However one explains the framework's pregnant omissions, it must be noted that the final narrative picture is one of the volunteering Israel letting God fight its battles and giving praise to those on Israel's margins. It is a picture of Israel not accused of idolatry but coming to its prophet to learn God's will. **It is Israel with a pair of leaders cooperating to let God bring blessing to his people** (emphasis added).[97]

If Jael is considered the ultimate human deliverer in Judges, and everything spirals downwards for Israel after the forty years of quiet, these facts can also apply to the Gospels' crucifixion and resurrection accounts: Jesus is the ultimate deliverer and that, while Israel has around forty years of quiet after the resurrection, everything goes downhill after that for Israel with the fall of Jerusalem in AD 70.

---

97. Butler, *Judges*, 171-72.

Conclusion

The Gospels' narrative pattern intertextuality functions to reveal that Jesus' crucifixion and resurrection fulfill God's ancient promises and prophecies. According to Richard Hays,

> The authors of our four canonical Gospels were the heirs of (the earliest Christian communities') tradition of storytelling, and they shared the early Christian community's passionate concern—a concern that, as far as we can tell, goes back to Jesus himself—to show that Jesus' teaching and actions, as well as his violent death and ultimate vindication, constituted the continuation and climax of the ancient biblical story (parenthetical added).[98]

The literary devices found in the intertextuality of these crucifixion and resurrection accounts include: a marker and marked text, reference to a doublet, biblical type-scene, powerful thematic imagery, quotation, images overlaying one another, *leitwort*, repetition, simile, ironic reversal, contrasting characters, and plot twist. And interestingly, the whole narrative of the Song of Deborah can be considered a prophetic word, given that Deborah authored it. It is this *whole narrative*, then, that prophetically foreshadows the crucifixion and resurrection narratives of Jesus' crushing the fountainhead of the Serpent who cruelly oppresses us and Jesus' rising from the dead. Although the poetic effect of metalepsis that results from the correspondence with the Jael texts in each readers' mind will be different, the *call to act* that results from the metalepsis will be the same.

Remaining circumspectly within the elements that the Gospels' crucifixion and resurrection narratives highlight, we can

---

98. Hays, *Echoes of Scripture in the Gospels*, 5.

draw several theological conclusions, even without examining how the Jael story initially fulfills Gen 3:15. Like Jael, God takes his tent peg—Jesus on the Cross—and drives it into the Evil One's skull, and it is crushed, shattered and pierced.[99] When observing the Gospels writers individually, it is apparent that Mark's Gospel has an emphasis upon God's victorious action in the Cross over moral and spiritual Darkness and Chaos. Luke keeps this idea, and for his more Gentile audience he adds the scene of Jesus counseling Jerusalem's ladies to be weeping for themselves, as the lesson would have been to Sisera's mother's ladies. Matthew recognizes God's actions in the three earthquakes, and has something distinctive to include about the command to lie at the guarding of the tomb. And John adds to the others' facets by revealing Jesus' substitutionary action in the Cross by seeing Jesus fulfilling Sisera's foretype in his receiving of the drink as well as Abimelech's foretype by being pierced in the side.

In terms of theological social justice, it can be noted that Jesus recognized the raping and trafficking of women, evidenced especially in his concern in Luke 23:27-31. The Lord now gives *us* the honor of working together with him to destroy this type of evil, as well as the evils of misogyny and sexism. At the very least, by retracting Jael's story Jesus identified with a woman's action as behind one meaning of his death. God looks over the whole story of the Old Testament and puts his finger on the story of Jael as one he wanted to converse about: the next chapter will discuss why.

---

99. See more below concerning this in the discussion on the "tent peg" in Zech 10:4.

TWO

THE *PROTOEVANGELIUM* PROMISE AND
THE JAEL STORY AS INITIAL FULFILLMENT

*Barak's (Deborah and Jael's) story points to a whole new kind of
"unforeseen situation" where God's sons and daughters fearlessly
join forces for his kingdom and end up praising God and singing
each other's praises because God is creating something new and the
kingdom of heaven is breaking in among us (parenthetical added).*
—Carolyn Custis James[100]

In their book written for the lay-person, *Christ from Beginning
to End: How the Full Story of Scripture Reveals the Full Glory of
Christ,* Trent Hunter and Stephen Wellum point out that the Old
Testament biblical authors use the typology of persons, events,
and institutions in non-accidental patterns which are picked up

---

100. Carolyn Custis James, *Maelstrom: Manhood Swept into the Currents of a Changing World* (Grand Rapids, MI: Zondervan, 2015), 111.

and repeated to show how God will keep his covenant promises, fulfilling them in the New Testament.[101] They also importantly claim that the short verse of Gen 3:15 is a "seed—a small promise that will eventually grow into the full-blown tree of God's good news, the storyline of Scripture,"[102] yet in their book they fail to recognize that the Jael story especially reveals the Gen 3:15 Edenic promise. This promise—the greatest promise of all—runs through the Old Testament as a beacon of hope. As Schreiner declares, "The seed of the woman runs from Abraham to David to Christ."[103] This chapter argues that the warrant for understanding the Jael story as a fulfillment narrative pattern behind the Gospels' crucifixion and resurrection accounts lies in the fact that the Jael story is an initial fulfillment of this *protoevangelium* promise. To accomplish this, the context of the two narratives will first be discussed before looking more fully at the common narrative elements between Gen 3:15, the Jael story, and the crucifixion and resurrection accounts.

Background of Gen 3:15 and the Jael Story

Translations of Gen 3:15 have been historically problematic. It is questioned whether it is a "he" that will bruise or crush the Serpent's head as the LXX has it or a "she" as Ambrose and the Latin Vulgate translates it or an "it" as in the King James Bible or even "they" as in the JPS Tanakh 1917. The translation is even made more confusing because, instead of the usual word

---

101. Trent Hunter and Stephen Wellum, *Christ from Beginning to End: How the Full Story of Scripture Reveals the Full Glory of Christ* (Grand Rapids, MI: Zondervan, 2018), 64-68.

102. Hunter and Wellum, *Christ from Beginning to End*, 95.

103. Schreiner, "Foundations for Faith," 3.

for "crushed" or "bruised," the LXX translates it with "keep" or "guard." Understanding the Genesis author's thoughts can be better attempted, therefore, through looking at the promise intertextually and theologically.

Augustine importantly asks about Gen 3:15, "Enmities are not set between the serpent and the man but between the serpent and the woman ... Hence, why does Scripture put it this way?"[104] His question is apt since Gen 3:15 refers to God setting a hostile distance between the serpent-figure and a *female* follower of Yahweh. Katherine Bushnell believed this verse to be saying that *woman* is not only the progenitor of the coming destroyer of Satan and his power but also, in her own person, Satan's enemy.[105] Bushnell also states, "It is not Adam, but the Word of God itself, that says Eve was '*the mother of all living*,'" and then she explains this by quoting Monroe Gibson, who says,

> Is it not quite obvious that "the seed of the woman" cannot mean all mankind, but simply those who are not only literally, but spiritually the "seed of the woman," those who are found on the side of good, the side of God and righteousness? Those who are of an opposite spirit are the seed of the serpent, "the children of the devil." ... So here, it is not only *I will put enmity*; but I am putting, and will put enmity between thee and the woman. The work is begun ... She is the first type and representative of all the separated ones who constitute the Church of God (*The Ages before Moses*, page 122).[106]

104. *Two Books on Genesis Against the Manichaeans* 2.18.28.
105. Bushnell, *God's Word to Women*, 43.
106. Bushnell, *God's Word to Women*, 36.

Considering the "living ones,"[107] the woman's seed then are those who are separated or holy unto God, which can be thought to be in keeping with the separations God makes in Gen 1.[108] However, it can be further clarifying to realize that the offspring of the serpent-figure—as will be shown in the New Testament—represent those exhibiting the ordinary state of all people who are not among the "separated ones" of the seed of the woman. Ronning rightly states that "'offspring of the serpent' is simply a way of saying they are unregenerate, which is the natural state of all people, not just Jews. Cain, the prototype of the offspring of the serpent, was obviously not Jewish."[109] *People* are not being demonized in this; recognition instead is made that there is a spiritual and moral force of evil in the world. Additionally, it is the woman's spiritual offspring—a male or female follower of Yahweh who is a representative for her seed—who crushes the *source* or *fountainhead*[110] of evil, represented by the serpent-figure. Witherington notes, "even in (God's judgment in Gen 3) there is mercy, because the seed of the woman will crush the head of evil and its source. This is poetic language and conjures up the image of evil snapping at our heels" (parenthetical added).[111] God promises to destroy the

107. Hunter and Wellum also question whether Eve's name as "mother of the living" might be "possibly related to God's promise." Hunter and Wellum, *Christ from Beginning to End*, 102.

108. Ronning, "Seven Keys."

109. Ronning, *The Jewish Targums*, 273.

110. Gilbert Bilezikian in referencing 1 Cor 11:3 says, "*head* has a meaning other than 'authority' in this passage, and it is a meaning that applies to a man and not to woman. The use of *head* as 'fountainhead' or 'supplier of life' resolves this difficulty, since Christ can be said to be the source of man's life, as man is the source of woman's life." Gilbert Bilezikian, *Beyond Sex Roles: What the Bible Says about a Woman's Place in Church and Family*, 3rd ed. (Grand Rapids, MI: Baker Academic, 2006), 227. I am indebted to Haley Gabrielle for alerting me to this reference.

111. Witherington, *Torah Old and New, 51*.

fountainhead of sin and death which hinders our relationship with him and prophesies of a coming rescuer that will restore humanity to God. Jesus' action begins this new covenantal relationship between the separated ones of the seed of the woman and God if they receive Jesus' action for them through faith. The rescuer destroys what keeps us from God—sin, death, and the devil—and in the *new* covenant proves God's renewal of his faithful love for humanity.

In terms of generally understanding Judges, it should first be noted that the Book of Judges is among the books of the Prophets rather than in the Torah or the Writings, and more specifically the Former Prophets instead of the Latter Prophets. This means that Deborah's prophecy in Judg 4:10 that "the Lord will sell Sisera into the hands of a woman" and her prophetic song narrative exhibit the same features that characterize those of the other prophets of the Lord. Hunter and Wellum see seven features of the Prophets of which the following are most pertinent to Deborah's ministry: "The prophets are God's authorized spokesmen," "the prophets speak in the context of the Law-covenant, which prescribed blessing for obedience and cursing for disobedience," and "the prophets share the same message of judgment and salvation ... (but) each prophetic voice is like a different ride in an amusement park, with its own turns and twists, scenes and surprises."[112]

The general context in Judg 4 and 5 indicates that Israel was experiencing immense oppression and a general lack of safety. Like the situation in the Good Samaritan parable, Block recognizes that "Israelite caravaneers have ceased to travel on their normal trade routes for fear of attack and/or extortionary tolls

---

112. Hunter and Wellum, *Christ from Beginning to End*, 173-75.

demanded at crossroads by the Canaanite oppressors."[113] He also notes, "Economic woes and enemy oppression threatened the growth of the population. In poetic hyperbole, Deborah sings, 'The peasant population disappeared in Israel.'"[114] This situation gives rise to their cry for God's help.

As for the Song of Deborah, it is ancient. According to Block, "Scholars are divided on questions of date and authorship of this ode. Most agree that—along with the Blessing of Jacob (Genesis 49), the Song of the Sea (Exodus 15), the oracles of Balaam (Numbers 23–24), and the Blessing of Moses (Deuteronomy 33)—Judges 5 ranks among the oldest monuments of Hebrew literature."[115] Butler notes that some see the Song of Deborah as being widely distributed and possibly used liturgically, stating that, "Within the complicated text history of the Greek texts of Judges, the text of the Song of Deborah suffered more than any other chapter probably because of its wide diffusion and possible liturgical use."[116] According to Arthur Cundall and Leon Morris, "In all probability it was included in one of the anthologies of poetry which existed in ancient Israel."[117] They go on to note, "The unit of Hebrew poetry is normally not the single line but the couplet, with a short pause at the end of the first line and a longer pause at the end of the second … This means that the association is one of thought not of sound, as in traditional English poetry; a mental picture is produced

---

113. Block, *Judges, Ruth*, 225.
114. Butler, *Judges*, 138.
115. Block, *Judges, Ruth*, 213.
116. Butler, *Judges*, 116n1.a. This comes from Tov (VT28 [1978] 225).
117. A. E. Cundall, and Leon Morris, *Judges and Ruth: An Introduction and Commentary* (Downers Grove, IL: InterVarsity Press, 1968), 91.

which is answered by another supplementary word-picture."[118] This means that since imagery was the important foundation within the structure of poetry itself, the similar imagery in the Song's intertextuality with Gen 3 is more important than it having the same rhymes and identical words. Brettler gives the tentative suggestion that the liturgical elements in the Song aren't "accretions but show that the song was meant to be used in religious contexts."[119] Butler notes other possible uses:

> Prior to battle, the song could muster the troops, encourage them, and promise assurance of victory by the God of the theophany. In times without imminent warfare, such a ritual could call the tribes of Israel to unity and perhaps covenant renewal. . . . Taken outside the cult into daily life, the song could encourage peasants in their daily struggles, call forth memories and songs of God's righteous acts in the past, and enhance patriotism and loyalty among the tribes.[120]

Given its widespread distribution, this much-loved Song is likely to have been used in all these ways. Block summarizes his analysis by stating that, "Most obviously, the ideal Israel is portrayed as the people of Yahweh, engaged in his service, committed to him in covenant love, and called upon to bless and praise him (vv. 2–3)."[121] This hymn was clearly crucial to Israel's identity and it can be supposed that it was therefore still well-known throughout New Testament times.

Regarding Barak, many scholars find him spineless; however, the New Testament has a different opinion: he is among

---

118. Cundall, *Judges and Ruth*, 92.
119. Butler, *Judges*, 132.
120. Ibid., 134.
121. Block, *Judges, Ruth*, 216.

those listed in Heb 11 as having great faith in God. Butler notes, "the editor's framework has Deborah and Barak sang together in that day, though the feminine singular verb form gives precedence to Deborah but gives no indication of a parody on General Barak."[122] And while often slandered about it as if he was too timid, it should instead be realized that Barak recognized the Lord's presence with Deborah when he says, "If you will go with me, I will go; but if you will not go with me, I will not go" (Judg 4:8). This is very similar to the statements Moses makes to God: "'Bring up this people,' but you have not let me know whom you will send with me…. If your presence will not go, do not carry us up from here." (Ex 33:12a, 15). Barak wanted God's prophet with him as Moses wanted God's angel. As Block accurately notes, "The request to be accompanied by the prophet is a plea for the presence of God."[123] He also sees, "The timing of Deborah's words is critical, for it occurs precisely at the point where, in other call narratives, Yahweh promises his personal presence to a reluctant agent. The prophet obviously functions as Yahweh's alter ego. Her presence alone is enough to guarantee victory over Sisera."[124] Pierce goes further, saying, "Barak acts as a man of faith who is willing to obey God's messenger, even if his personal glory is not part of the reward."[125] This reveals that Barak is accepting the prophet's description of what will take place, which proves him to be a humble servant of God who is not obeying God for his personal glory.

---

122. Butler, *Judges*, 136.

123. Block, *Judges, Ruth*, 199.

124. Ibid., 200.

125. Pierce, "Deborah," 4.

As was seen previously, if the Kenite Jael is the Book of Judges' ultimate human deliverer, "Israel is now identified through the actions and attitudes of their fringe members not their core constituency," says Butler.[126] But who is Jael? It is questioned whether either Deborah or Jael were married. John Goldingay recognizes that, as "Lappidot" means "torches," "flames," or "flashes" and is a feminine word, it would be strange to use it for the name of a man, and "'heber' is most often an ordinary word meaning 'company,' and Ya'el may simply be described as 'the woman who belongs to the Qenite group.'"[127] Translating then, Deborah can be a woman of flame and Jael a woman of the community of the Kenites.

If Jael *is* married to Heber, then she—like Abigail—works against her husband, who has foolishly aligned himself with King Jabin. Furthermore, Jael's motivation to kill Sisera is not given. Jael herself is a non-Israelite woman, though, who has chosen Israel's side and become their unexpected heroine, like Ruth and Rahab were. According to Younger, "Jael would not typically be expected to get involved. Not only is she unrelated to the warring parties, but normally would be about her pacific feminine, tent-dwelling duties. But she has risked everything to execute the enemy of God and to aid God's people."[128] He goes on to state, "The poem paints Jael in terms of the head-smashing, victorious monarch. Consequently, her praiseworthy deed can be described in terms of the victorious conquering leader—and not just a conqueror of Sisera but everything embodied in him,

---

126. Butler, *Judges*, 154.
127. Goldingay, "Motherhood, Machismo," 23, 29.
128. Younger, *Judges and Ruth*, 154.

the enemy Canaanites."[129] If Jael was seen as a "head-smashing victorious monarch" this would align well with Jesus as a victorious monarch through embodying her story, as well show him fulfilling the Gen 3:15 promise and victoriously crushing the fountainhead of the Serpent.

Lastly, there may be an allusion to Jael's victory in Zech 10:4: "Out of them shall come the cornerstone, out of them **the tent peg**, out of them the battle bow, out of them every commander" (emphasis added). The tent peg imagery from this verse may not appear clearly in the New Testament given that the LXX eliminates it: "And from it he took perspective, and from it he drew up in battle order, and from it was a bow with fury; from it everyone who marches out will come together" (NETS, Zech 10:4). However there are many instances of the allusion to Jesus as the *cornerstone* in the New Testament.[130] Also, N. T. Wright in *Jesus and the Victory of God* contends that *Zechariah* had a great influence on Jesus, particularly chapters 9-14: "Israel are like sheep without a shepherd (10:2); they have shepherds but they are not doing their job, and will be punished (10:3) as part of the divine plan for the return from exile (10:6-12)."[131] The citation of "one whom they have pierced" from Jn 19:37 is in Zech 12:10, too, and Jesus quotes Zech 9:9 in Jn 12:15. Thus, it is not unlikely that Jesus saw himself as God's "tent peg" from Zech 10:4.

---

129. Ibid., 155.

130. Matt 21:42; Mk 12:10, 11; Luke 20:17; Acts 4:11; Eph 2:20; 1 Pet 2:4, 6.

131. N. T. Wright, *Jesus and the Victory of God* (Minneapolis, MN: Fortress Press, 1996), 586.

The Common Elements of Gen 3:15 and the Jael Story

The narrative elements and motifs of Gen 3 illustrate that there are many similarities between Gen 3 and the Jael story. Although she doesn't acknowledge narrative patterns, Cynthia Edenburg recognizes seven literary features that signify possible intertextuality to an audience: a common formal structure, common motifs, doublets, variant accounts, text commenting on a previous text that explains or actualizes a text, indirect allusions, and direct quotes.[132] These were all evident in the previous chapter in the crucifixion and resurrection accounts' intertextual references to the Jael story. The intertextuality between Gen 3 and the Jael story also exhibit all of these literary features, except for direct quotes. Although the Song of Deborah is thought to be older than the written text of Genesis, Judges 5 may be an initial fulfillment and expansion upon an oral tradition of the Genesis text. Jeffrey Leonard states, "It has long been recognized that the literature of the Hebrew Bible was composed not as large, discrete blocks but as a succession of layers built one on another. What Fishbane and others have made apparent is that these strata become interwoven as later biblical authors allude to and then reconfigure earlier layers of tradition."[133] The Gen 3 narrative, the Jael story, and allusions to both of them in the Gospels share many obvious common elements: a poetry format, a serpent-figure, deception, mothers, seed/offspring of a woman, seed/offspring of a Serpent, striking/ crushing a head, a skull, enmity between the Serpent and his

---

132. Edenburg, "How (Not) to Murder a King," 64-71.

133. Jeffery Leonard, "Inner-Biblical Interpretation and Intertextuality," in *Literary Approaches to the Bible*, ed. by Douglas Mangum and Douglas Estes (Bellingham, WA: Lexham Press, 2017), 109.

spiritual children and a woman and her spiritual children, and a curse and blessing. These correspondences will be discussed in three groupings below.

A mother—as "woman"—and her spiritual children. Gen 3:15, the Jael story, and the Gospels' texts all comment on female characters being specifically a "woman." Pierce identifies:

> Deborah is introduced dramatically as the story's main character with a string of seven consecutive, grammatically feminine words: her proper name followed by three paired terms. She is "Deborah," (1) a "woman, a prophet" (fem. nouns), (2) "a woman of light/fire" (fem. nouns), and (3) "she herself, she is judging" (fem. pronoun, fem. participle).[134]

The Judges author is clearly making a point about Deborah being a woman. Jael's blessing in Judg 5:24 similarly includes two references to her as a woman, and the dialogue of chauvinistic Abimelech's desire to not be killed by "a woman" in the Jael doublet story of Judg 9 was also mentioned previously. It can be maintained that that there is clear intertextuality in this with Gen 3:15 because they specifically note "woman."

Correspondingly, concerning Jesus calling his mother "woman," the editors of *Mary in the New Testament* state, "There is no precedent in Hebrew or, to the best of our knowledge, in Greek, for a son to address his mother thus; and so most scholars have detected a special significance in the term."[135] They go on to propose that "the two Johannine scenes in which Mary is addressed as 'Woman' may be seen as a reenactment of the

---

134. Pierce, "Deborah," 3.

135. Raymond E. Brown, et al., eds., *Mary in the New Testament: A Collaborative Assessment by Protestant and Roman Catholic Scholars* (New York: Paulist Press, 1978), 188.

Eve motif with a happier ending."[136] Moreover, they suggest that since Jesus addressed the Samaritan woman and Mary Magdalene in the same way, Jesus might not have placed any special emphasis upon Mary's physical motherhood.[137] It appears to be Jesus' normal way of addressing women.[138] It can also be argued that Jesus was alluding to the Jael story and his Gen 3:15 mission throughout his ministry, as will be further developed below.

Gen 3:15, Judg 5:24, and Luke 1:42b—foreshadowing for Luke his story of the atonement—also have much in common. First, given that parallelism is a hallmark of Hebrew poetry, they share the same genre. "BHS says 'the wife of Heber the Kenite' is an addition from 4:17,"[139] which would make the resemblance to Judg 5:24 in Luke 1:42 even stronger.[140] Younger recognizes the allusion, saying, "The unrestrained praise of Jael is analogous to that given to Mary in Luke 1:42."[141] McCann claims:

> That Jael, like the later monarchs, is portrayed as **an embodiment of God's will for justice and righteousness** explains why she is called "most blessed of women" (v. 24). This designation anticipates Elizabeth's proclamation to Mary—who has been told that she will bear a royal child

---

136. Brown, *Mary in the New Testament*, 190.

137. Ibid., 189. See also J. Kottackal, "Mary in the Bible," *Bible Bhashyam* 25, no. 2 (1999): 140-41, accessed August 15, 2017, New Testament Abstracts, EBSCOhost.

138. See Matt 15:28, 11:11; Lk 7:28, 13:12; 22:57; Jn 2:4, 4:21, 8:10, 19:26, 20:13.

139. Butler, *Judges*, 121n24.a.

140. It can also be recognized that in the deuterocanonical novelette *Judith* Uzziah the high priest declares Judith "blessed by the most high God above all women on earth; and blessed be the Lord God who created the heavens and the earth, who has guided you to strike the head of our enemies" (Jth 13:18). Judith is called by the people "the great glory of Israel" (15:9). This can be a reference to both Judg 5:24 and Gen 3:15.

141. Younger, *Judges and Ruth*, 154.

("Son of God" in Luke 1:35 is a royal title; see Ps. 2:7)—
"Blessed are you among women" (Luke 1:42). Not coinci-
dentally, Mary proceeds immediately to sing a song, the
Magnificat, which, like the Song of Deborah and Barak,
celebrates God's defeat of oppressors (emphasis added).[142]

This blessing then causes McCann to liken Jael to Mary, as they
are both chosen by God to defeat God's Enemy, establishing
justice and righteousness. Secondly, like Deborah, Elizabeth
can also be seen as a type of "mother in Israel" (Judg 5:7) since
she was in the lineage of Aaron and the wife of the priest Zechariah, as well as being the mother of John the Baptist. Therefore
Deborah and Mary both echo the spiritual mother of the offspring of Gen 3:15. Thirdly, like Deborah, Elizabeth filled with
the Holy Spirit also prophesies about Mary and the "mother of
my Lord." In addition, the Luke 1:42b allusion to Judg 5:24 and
Gen 3:15 functions to identify Jesus' lineage with the Woman's
line over the Serpent's line and foreshadows that the Gen 3:15
promise will be fulfilled and that the offspring of *this woman*
shall be the one to strike the head of the enemy. Ron Pierce and
Rebecca Groothuis go further and state, "The whole point of
the virginal conception and birth was that Christ was the 'seed'
of both God and Mary (Gen 3:15; Is 53:10)."[143] Lastly, Goldingay also sees that both Deborah and Jael act as independent
women,[144] which can also be said of Elizabeth in her prophe-
sying and Mary in her conception, given that neither consulted
with men beforehand.

142. McCann, *Judges*, 58.

143. Ronald W. Pierce and Rebecca Merrill Groothuis, eds., *Discovering Biblical
Equality: Complementary Without Hierarchy*, 2nd ed. (Downers Grove: IVP Academic,
2005), 297.

144. Goldingay, "Motherhood, Machismo," 29.

A serpent-figure and his spiritual children. Regarding Gen 3:15, Katherine Bushnell wrote, "Not only is it prophesied that her seed should be at enmity with Satan, but *woman herself* shall wage war with Satan."[145] This hostility between the serpent-figure and women can be most specifically seen in the hostility between the serpent-figure Sisera and Jael and chauvinistic Abimelech and women. Sisera, analogously, is a spiritual "offspring" of King Jabin, who had cruelly oppressed Israel, a region that Deborah was leading, for twenty years (Judg 4:3). One distinct conclusion of Judg 9 is that offspring of the Serpent think less of women than they do of men, given also Jacob Wright's understanding mentioned earlier of one of Judges moral standards being how a people treat its women. Abimelech has a sexist attitude, in contrast to Israel, which was blessed with women leaders in their society as judges and in their religion as prophets. This revelation can be similarly correlated with the male-led society and the male-led priesthood of Israel and their antagonism with Jesus.

Jesus also frequently identifies the Serpent's offspring when he refers to Pharisees, Sadducees, crowds or others as a "brood of vipers"—"offspring of serpents" in other words—or something similar, like "from your father the devil" (see Mt 3:7, 12:34, 13:37-39, 23: 33; Lk 3:7, Jn 8:44, Acts 13:10, and 1 Jn 3:8-10; cf. with *his* seed in Mk 16:18; Lk 10:19, and Rom 3:13). Moreover, as Michael Green makes it clear, Jesus saw his whole life as fighting against Satan. "He saw the whole of his ministry as a conflict with Satan. He saw his death as the supreme battle with the evil one."[146] Jesus realized that he was tempted by Satan in

---

145. Bushnell, *God's Word to Women*, 350.
146. Michael Green, *I Believe in Satan's Downfall*, 3rd ed. (London: Hodder and Stoughton, 1995), 28.

the wilderness, Satan snatched away the good news from those listening, Satan sowed tares in God's field, and Satan usurped God's place of leadership in the world. Jesus also taught his disciples to pray for deliverance from the evil one and saw himself as the one who needed to bind the strong man.[147] Green notes, "rather than compromise with the subtle and evil force, Jesus knows that he must oppose him to the bitter end. Hence the way of the cross."[148] This was the only way Satan could finally be defeated.

Hamilton finds an allusion to Gen 3:15 in Luke when he translates 10:19 as "Behold, I have given to you the authority to tread upon snakes and scorpions, and upon all the power of the one who is at enmity."[149] Jesus' spiritual offspring, the seventy, have authority over the Serpent, who is at enmity with them. It can be suggested that in this pericope Jesus is also alluding to more than just Gen 3:15. Jesus states, "I **watched Satan fall** from heaven like a flash of lightning" at the ministry of his seventy in 10:18 (emphasis added). This may be an echo of Deborah's prophecy with the serpent-figure Sisera falling to the feet of Jael: "He sank, he fell, he lay still at her feet; at her feet he sank, he fell; where he sank, there he fell dead" (Judg 5:27). This, besides the Luke 1:42b allusion, would then be more foreshadowing of his Jael story work at Golgotha where the Serpent will fall dead at Jesus' feet. It also correlates the similar work of Jesus' followers to Jesus himself. Pedro Calderón de la Barca, as mentioned previously, also connected Satan's fall from heaven and Sisera's fall to Jael's feet.

---

147. Green, *I Believe in Satan's Downfall*, 26.
148. Ibid.
149. Hamilton, "The Skull Crushing Seed of the Woman," 42.

McCann claims that the Judg 4 and 5 defeat of King Jabin and Sisera is similar to the exodus which brought a renewal of creation:

> The episode is not merely a local action against Jabin and Sisera; rather, it is part of a larger trajectory that begins with creation, includes the exodus, and later will include *God's defeat of Israel itself* when its kings turn out to be oppressors like Pharaoh, Jabin, and Sisera. The shape and movement of the Book of Judges, along with the larger canonical context, reveal that God shows no partiality to Israel as such. Rather, God is partial to justice and righteousness, which means that God opposes oppressors.[150]

Oppression is at odds with the new creation God desires to bring forth. Similarly, when the Israelite institutional systems of the Scribes and Pharisees lead to oppression, God stands against them and brings liberation.

A curse on the Enemy and blessing on one who crushes the Enemy of the Lord. Phyllis Trible recognizes in Gen 3, "When he was enticing the couple to disobey, the serpent spoke specifically to the woman but, through the use of plural pronouns, included the man also. Accordingly, the curse upon this animal continues with an explicit refence to the woman that also involves the man (3:15);" and Trible sees that the Serpent "having spoken to the woman as the representative of the human couple, he now lives in hostility with the woman and her offspring."[151] In other words, the Serpent dealt with the woman as the representative of both humans, and God took the same

---

150. McCann, *Judges*, 60.

151. Phyllis Trible, *God and the Rhetoric of Sexuality* (Philadelphia: Fortress Press, 1978), 124-25.

approach when he cursed the Serpent: his people had "the woman" as their representative.

In Judg 5 Meroz, who has not come to help Yahweh, is cursed, while Jael, who did help Yahweh, is blessed. According to Younger, "The transition of the curse of Meroz (Strophe 14) is pronounced by the angel (or messenger, *mal'ak*) of Yahweh (5:23; cf. 2:1). The repetition of the imperative 'curse' and the reintroduction of the divine name, Yahweh, disclose the poet's point of view clearly: Every soldier, battalion, or community that commits himself/itself to warfare is helping Yahweh; all are needed."[152] Trent Butler adds, "Meroz is central to the repeated theme of blessing on freewill volunteering, battle participation, and personal initiative to defeat the enemy contrasted to cursing on those who do not participate and thus show love for Yahweh."[153] Volunteerism is key to the blessing, even if it comes from non-Israelite women such as Jael.

Therefore, intertextuality between Gen 3:14-15 and Judg 5:23-24 can be observed. There is a curse upon Meroz, as there is the curse upon the Serpent in Gen 3:14. There is also a blessing upon Jael, who is an unstated *spiritual offspring* of Deborah, as there is an implied blessing upon the woman's offspring in Gen 3:15 in the promise to crush the Serpent's head. A repetition of this curse and blessing in Judg 5:31 can also be seen as another allusion to Gen 3:15. God's enemies are like Meroz, and God's friends are like Jael. Within the curse and blessing of Judg 5:23-24, John Ronning also perceives a type of reverse fall narrative in Judg 4, stating,

---

152. Younger, *Judges and Ruth*, 153.

153. Butler, *Judges*, 154.

As predicted in the curse, we see the introduction of enmity between the seed of the woman (here also a woman) and the seed of the serpent, Sisera. Deborah calls Jael תְּבֹרַךְ מִנָּשִׁים "blessed among women" (Judg 5:24), which in the immediate context is a contrast to the cursed inhabitants of Meroz who would not join the battle (Judg 5:23), but also recalls (in contrast) the beginning of the curse on the serpent, "אָרוּר ... מִכָּל־הַבְּהֵמָה, cursed ... above all beasts" (Gen 3:14). The contrast between Jael and the inhabitants of Meroz suggests that Jael acted from spiritual motives, thus as a true seed of the woman. In Genesis 3 the serpent deceived the woman to bring about her downfall; here the woman deceives the serpent's seed to bring about his downfall.[154]

Jael *does* succeed where Eve failed; she disregards the serpent-figure's instructions and kills him instead. However, the older, prophetic interpretation of the event in Deborah's Song does not equally have the idea of Jael being deceptive. In Deborah's Song Jael is the godly hero, so Jael as deceptive is not what is being emphasized. Younger declares, "With intensity equal to that of the curse of Meroz, blessing is proclaimed for Jael. In fact, she is made the receiving end of blessing, which is given to only one other character in the poem, God himself!"[155] Therefore, it can be argued that Jael receives a blessing because she fulfills the Gen 1:28 joint vocation to properly steward creation: Jael exercised her dominion over the Serpent in contrast to Eve (and Adam) who did not.

---

154. Ronning, "The Curse on the Serpent," 294.
155. Younger, *Judges and Ruth*, 154.

Conclusion

This chapter has shown that the Gen 3:15 Edenic covenant was begun in the Garden with the woman. It was then initially fulfilled with Deborah and Jael in Judges 4 and 5. In terms of Edenburg's seven literary features signifying intertextuality to an audience—a common formal structure, common motifs, doublets, variant accounts, text commenting on a previous text that explains or actualizes a text, indirect allusions, and direct quotes—all but the last are seen between these two Old Testament texts.[156] They both have a poetry structure. The Jael story has the doublet story in Judges 9 with another woman crushing the skull of a different serpent-figure. There are slightly variant accounts of the Jael story in the narrative version and in the poetic Song of Deborah, yet both retain the important main features of Gen 3:15. The Jael story *actualizes* the Gen 3:15 promise. And the main indirect allusions to Gen 3:15 in Judges 4 and 5 include: a serpent-figure, deception, mothers, seed/offspring of a woman, seed/offspring of a Serpent, striking/crushing a head, a skull, enmity between the Serpent and his spiritual children and a woman and her spiritual children, a curse and a blessing.

The Jael story, therefore, supplies a rich apologetic for the Cross. There are God-designed patterns within the Jael story that link with the *protoevangelium* and illuminate Christ to us. God enacted the Good News beforehand in the story of Jael so that we would recognize it when it came. This story reveals the deliverance of the Cross, of which the deliverance that Jael brought was only a foretype, fulfilling the ancient promise of

---

156. Edenburg, "How (Not) to Murder a King," 64-71.

God to crush the Evil One. The hero here is the Kenite Jael, a foreigner. She is not known as a mother, or even necessarily as a wife,[157] therefore it is not her relationship status that is being emphasized—only her singular action. She stands up for God's interests and God's glory. Likewise, the blessing of the Good News has a universal scope with an offer to all ethnicities. And God's blessings come upon cultures with women as leaders in society and when they are prophets and leaders in God's movement like Deborah.

Christlike ones such as Jael—those who love God and shine like the marching out of the sun—are those also courageously exhibiting a monarch-like rule over creation as God's image-bearers, especially subduing the evil emanating from "the sliest of all the wild beasts that Yahweh God had made" (Gen 3:1).[158] They have God's rule in mind and thus exercise their male or female joint-vocation mandate from God to properly steward the earth. They are the characters of the New Creation. As Origen saw it, God uses the Cross as the tent peg through them to destroy his enemy. They crush the fountainhead of evil, especially witnessed in oppression and lack of safety. Salvation comes through rescue and brings a renewal of creation. In this they are following Jesus, their representative head as the offspring of the woman, who spent his life fighting evil and bringing rescue. We, too, can become God's tent pegs as we live in him.

---

157. Ron Pierce also notes the understanding of *heber* as a common collective noun by A. Malmat and J.A. Soggin and Johannna W. H. Bos." Ronald W. Pierce, "Deborah," 7n23.

158. This is Phyllis Trible's translation. Trible, *God and the Rhetoric of Sexuality*, 106.

CONCLUSION

The reason the Son of God appeared was to destroy the works of the devil.

—1 John 3:8

Summary

The powerful fusion of the events of the crucifixion and resurrection of Jesus Christ combined together with the fulfillment narrative pattern of the literalistic fulfillment of Gen 3:15 in the Jael story results in the following summation description that has an explicit apologetic for the Cross. Jesus, as the second person of the Trinity, came to Golgotha as a sign of what was about to happen in the dark spiritual realm. At the Skull, God hammered the nail of the Cross down into the realm of chaos, obscured understandings, spiritual and moral darkness, inner slavery to sin, and victimization by evil. On God's tent peg Jesus said, "I am thirsty," showing that he is an offering for the sins of even the archetypal evil Sisera, commander of God's enemy's army. The Roman soldiers thought they were dividing the spoils of Jesus' death; however, women especially were instead receiving their spiritual freedom from domination and abuse as a result of Jesus' death. Jesus died for all to become regenerated in him through faith. Jesus even died out of love for chauvinistic Abimelech, which is proved when the soldier pierces him through with his sword. Earthquakes happened when God marched out at Jesus' death, opening both the veil to himself and people's eyes to Jesus as God's Son and then, once again, when God resurrected Jesus Christ. Humans can try to keep people imprisoned under tyranny and oppression, but God subdued the Serpent, and his righteous friends shine like the sun as they, along with the resurrected Jesus, rescue people from darkness and Satan's grip. God's "living ones" in his new creation in the Church of Jesus Christ therefore now sing as Deborahs, Baraks, and Jaels together in praise.

This narrative pattern intertextuality is especially proved by the cumulative effect of multiple allusions, as well as by closely following the Jael story's actual sequence of events. The literary marker of intertextuality, the narrative elements, the Jael story's doublet in the woman with the millstone, the general order of events, and the plot twist in the empty tomb are all present in the Gospels' crucifixion and resurrection accounts. As Ben Witherington says, "The long arc of the story of creation, human sin, and alienation from God, and of God's various acts of redemption and restoration, provides the framework out of which particular Old Testament narratives are drawn on by Jesus and the writers of the New Testament."[159]

Literary criticism declares that it is impossible to control the metalepsis people will do: the parts of the Jael story that will stand out to them will be determined individually and in their

---

159. Witherington, *Torah Old and New*, 36.

community. However the elements highlighted in the cruci-fixion and resurrection stories will likely be the focus of atten-tion. The forceful resulting metalepsis exhorts the audience to likewise destroy the work of God's enemy in the world. The offspring of the woman are called to crush the fountainhead of evil. This theological understanding also makes it very clear that God's people are not at war with non-Christians: people are never to be demonized, although they do have agency when they choose to cooperate with the devil.

Scholars often facily assert that Jesus has crushed Satan at the Cross in the Gospels, but usually they cannot do it with-out resorting to quotes mostly from the Epistles. This study has discussed how the fulfillment narrative pattern of the Jael story being the back-story of the Gospel accounts explains how Jesus actually accomplished this theologically. Green states, "Satan has lain under judgment since Eden. The judgment was imple-mented on Calvary. The sentence passed on Satan in Genesis 3 has been executed."[160] God's *protoevangelium* covenant prom-ise in Gen 3:15 is that the offspring of the woman would crush Satan's head. The fact that Jesus accomplished this is seen by his fulfillment of Jael's prophetic sign-act in Judg 4 and Deb-orah's prophetic Song, which is an actualization and a type of reverse fall narrative of Gen 3:15, where Jael disobeys the ser-pent-figure and crushes his head instead, exercising her creation mandate to steward the earth including God's wiliest creature, Satan. For those who love God, this type of spiritual action is an expression of their love for him.

One might expect the fulfilled promises of God and the allusions to the Old Testament to occur one on top of the other

---

160. Green, *I Believe in Satan's Downfall*, 49.

in the narratives of the Cross and Resurrection. As Green states, "behind the cross there lay the predestination of God. If God ever acted in history, he acted then."[161] So Jesus' statement of "I am thirsty" in Jn 19:28 can be a reference to both Ps 69:21 and Judg 4:19. And Jesus dies as the Suffering Servant of Isaiah and in the place of Sisera as a sin offering. The reference "they will look on the one whom they have pierced" in Jn 19:37 can allude to both Zech 12:10 and Judg 9:54, as Jesus stood in the place of Abimelech. Jesus can also be both God's cornerstone of Zech 10:4 and his tent peg. In Jesus, God has finally fulfilled all his promises. As chaos and moral and spiritual darkness gained the ascendancy, the Father used his Son on the Cross as a tent peg to crush their Fountainhead. We in Christ are now involved in what N.T. Wright terms "the mopping-up operation." Christ has fulfilled all the promises of God, and in Him we are now bringing all of them more fully into fruition.

The Gospels' fulfillment narrative pattern of the Jael story also reveals a resurrection community of those who love God, as the Song of Deborah implies Jael did. Similarly to the Lukan beatitudes, however, "all the 'wrong' people are 'in' and all the 'right' people are 'out.'"[162] The women who are going to Jesus' burial site out of love for him are like the Kenite Jael and so they are "in," while chauvinistic Abimelech and the religious leaders who are commanding a guard to be placed in front of the tomb are "out." Volunteerism, heart attitude and obedience to Christ are key. Yet—Jesus drank Sisera's cup (Judg 4:19, Jn 19:28) and was pierced for the transgressions of chauvinistic Abimelech

161. Green, *I Believe in Satan's Downfall*, 94.

162. Scot McKnight, *The King Jesus Gospel*, 97.

(Judg 9:54, Jn 19:37). Therefore, Sisera and Abimelech are all of us. The love of God has been poured out unconditionally, and those in his family who receive it are those who also receive God's blessing through it.

Given this intertextuality, when an audience of the Gospel narratives that know the Old Testament story of Jael hear the account of Jesus' crucifixion and resurrection, they should have a *déjà vu* experience of Israel's ancient worship song—the Song of Deborah and its narrative—which celebrate God's coming deliverance of his people before it even happens. This same song is now being sung by Christ's people of their deliverance that was inaugurated at Golgotha in the cross and resurrection of Jesus. This exodus out of Sin's slavery is portrayed as a renewal of creation because where God is exercising his rulership, Satan and his despotism get dethroned.

Implications

The impacts of this study upon mission could be wide-ranging. Paradoxically, Green notes, "doubt about the existence of a malign focus of evil is to be found, by and large, only in Christian lands;" Animism, Islam, and Hinduism acknowledge a great Enemy.[163] The conclusions of this study then could have immense influence upon mission to those in non-Western cultures and to those in these religions by clearly showing how Jesus has defeated this evil force at the Cross. For cultures and religions that are complementarian, this study's revelations of gender equality could also have far-reaching effects. God's

---

163. Green, *I Believe in Satan's Downfall*, 17.

action at the Cross brings humanity back into the Edenic blessing and joint-vocation of Gen 1:28, where women and men
are allies. The Old Testament's male and female storylines—
threads of prefigured redemption—are brought together at
the Cross into Christ, the Great Reconciliation. The Kenite
Jael, a non-Israelite, being the hero shows that neither racism
nor sexism belong in either God's house or society in general.
One's gender or ethnicity neither precludes nor privileges a
person from serving in any way in the family of God—a new
day has begun in Christ.

Within the Jael story, too, there is a recognition that in every
conflict of war women are raped, if not trafficked. Women, as
the Serpent's great adversary, have suffered more of the world's
injustice. And Jesus gave his life standing against this evil. Yet
he doesn't view women as victims; he sees and encourages their
agency. Women are essential to God's plan of redemption as
Deborah sings, "until I Deborah arose as a mother in Israel."
Oppression reigned *until* she arose. As Katherine Bushnell recognized, there are some problems in the world that only Christ's
women can solve.[164] In her biography of Bushnell, Kristin Kobes
Du Mez states, "Despite the disappointments (Bushnell) had
encountered, however, she remained certain that Christ was
'the great emancipator of women,' and that 'if women were
given their God-ordained place in the church, Christendom
would expand in breadth and height of influence.'"[165] Proving
this, God uses Deborah to bring his justice and righteousness.
Likewise, against the male-led system of the Pharisees, Scribes
and Roman soldiers, God uses the Jael story as a fulfillment

---

164. Bushnell, *God's Word to Women*, 6.
165. Kristin Kobes Du Mez, *A New Gospel for Women: Katharine Bushnell and the*

narrative pattern behind the Cross. Thereby God puts his endorsement and affirmation upon the New Creation's religious leadership that includes Deborahs and Jaels, Elizabeths and Marys.

Likewise, God's method to shape us into his image is inextricably linked with Jesus' mission in the world to free it from Satan's hold and reunite it with God's plan for a flourishing, New Creation. Similarly, Jesus' community is supposed to be a symbolic representation of the Good News, and therefore women's leadership within the community is a "gospel issue" and not a "women's issue." As Christ is the Great Reconciliation, his body should be as well with women and men co-laboring as one.

So why has the Church tended to disregard the stories of women such as Deborah and Jael in Scripture? Goldingay believes:

> It is not merely that the Church has tended to prefer men's stories in Scripture, though that is so. It is that the violence of stories such as (Deborah's) and Ya'el's, or Ehud's and Shamgar's, makes us feel uncomfortable. It places us with the fact of violence within ourselves, which we prefer to avoid. But it also seems at tension with the sense expressed elsewhere in Scripture that the solution to violence issues from letting it be done to oneself, not doing it.[166]

Violence is not solved by more violence, but only through the Cross, where the world's violence was spent upon Jesus. Yet people often overlook a man's violent actions such as the brave, young David who decapitates Goliath and then marches

---

Challenge of Christian Feminism (New York: Oxford University Press, 2015), 180.

166. Goldingay, "Motherhood, Machismo," 23, 29.

around with Goliath's head in his hand (1 Sam 17). Many are more squeamish about a similarly disgusting story involving a woman. Like the crucifixion, though, David's and Jael's actions are gruesome spectacles, but these violent events were needed for God to bring his deliverance. And God marks off his people as those who are known through crushing the Serpent's head, despite our culture's sensitivities regarding this imagery.

Another conclusion of this study recognizes that Jesus saw identification with a woman's action as the meaning of his death. And Deborah's Song is addressed to the kings of the world. Therefore, ministries supporting and empowering women and mothers in general—anti-trafficking work, micro-financing of women's projects, the property rights of women, pro-life work and pro-life centers' support of new mothers, the education of girls, eliminating child marriages, supporting women in ministry and theological education, reducing rape, domestic abuse and violence—touch both the heart of God and embody Jesus' acted-upon mission at the Cross.

The implications of this study also show that a virtuous woman looks like the strong, resourceful, and courageous Jael. Compassion, action for another's plight and the courage to live out of one's comfort zone are at the core of the Jael story. Jael didn't need to get involved with Israel's problems with King Jabin, as her tribe had a covenant with him. Like the Good Samaritan, she risked her neck to heal a problem not hers. "The Bible, from its opening chapters, pictures woman as allied with God, in the eventual salvation of the world," states Bushnell.[167] Similarly, the Cross shows us that it is not necessarily a Moses or a David but a Jael, an ordinary person using the day's

---

167. Bushnell, *God's Word to Women*, 33.

opportunities, who will bring God's deliverance to people. Jesus humbly lived into *her* story. Jael's actions are like a window on heaven, through which one can see what life and worship are like there. Yet, Christlikeness is not about Jael herself, but more about her being a representative of the people of God who love him and his ways.

It is possible that Jesus, who preached that the Son of Man did not come to be served but to serve, saw himself serving the lowliest, such as the non-Israelite woman Jael, by becoming her servant, her tent peg: in Jesus' kingdom, the humble are exalted. It is also possible to see God in the place of Jael, embodying her story and using his Son to hammer his enemy. And it is possible to see Jesus embodying the enemy Sisera's story and becoming an offering for the sin of us all. At the very least, Jesus chose Jael's story as the one he especially wanted his Church to discuss. It was *her* story that held his heart.

May those who love him be like the mighty sun as it rises.
(Judg 5:31)

BIBLIOGRAPHY

Alter, Robert. *The Art of Biblical Narrative*. Basic Books, 1981.

Arndt, W., F. W. Danker, W. Bauer, and F. W. Gingrich. *A Greek-English Lexicon of the New Testament and Other Early Christian Literature*. 3rd ed. Chicago: University of Chicago Press, 2000.

Ben-Porat, Ziva. "The Poetics of Literary Allusion." *PTL: A Journal for Descriptive Poetics and Theory of Literature* 1 (1976): 105–128.

Bilezikian, Gilbert. *Beyond Sex Roles: What the Bible Says about a Woman's Place in Church and Family*. 3rd ed. Grand Rapids, MI: Baker Academic, 2006.

Block, Daniel I. *Judges, Ruth*. Nashville: Broadman & Holman Publishers, 1999.

Brown, Jeannine K. "Metalepsis." In *Exploring Intertextuality: Diverse Strategies for New Testament Interpretation of Texts*, edited by B. J. Oropeza and Steve Moyise, 29-41. Eugene, OR: Cascade Books, 2016.

Brown, Raymond E., Karl P. Donfried, Joseph A. Fitzmyer, and John Reumann, eds. *Mary in the New Testament: A Collaborative Assessment by Protestant and Roman Catholic Scholars*. New York: Paulist Press, 1978.

Butler, Trent C. *Judges, Volume 8*. Grand Rapids, MI: Zondervan, 2009.

Cundall, A. E. and Morris, L. *Judges and Ruth: An Introduction and Commentary*. Downers Grove, IL: InterVarsity Press, 1968.

Du Mez, Kristin Kobes. *A New Gospel for Women: Katharine Bushnell and the Challenge of Christian Feminism*. New York: Oxford University Press, 2015.

Edenburg, Cynthia. "How (Not) to Murder a King: Variations on a Theme in 1 Sam 24; 26." *Scandinavian Journal of the Old Testament* 12, no.1 (1998): 64-85.

Franke, J. R. ed. *Old Testament IV: Joshua, Judges, Ruth, 1–2 Samuel.* Downers Grove, IL: InterVarsity Press, 2005.

Goldingay, John. "Motherhood, Machismo, and the Purpose of Yahweh in Judges 4-5." *Anvil* 12, no. 1, (1995): 21-33.

Green, Michael. *I Believe in Satan's Downfall.* 3rd ed. London: Hodder and Stoughton, 1995.

Hamilton, James M. "The Skull Crushing Seed of the Woman: Inner-Biblical Interpretation of Genesis 3: 15." *Southern Baptist Journal of Theology* 10, no. 2 (2006): 30-54. Accessed September 19, 2017. http://equip.sbts.edu/wp-content/uploads/2010/07/sbjt _102_sum06-hamilton.pdf.

Hays, Richard B. *Echoes of Scripture in the Gospels.* Waco, TX: Baylor University Press, 2016.

–––––. *Echoes of Scripture in the Letters of Paul.* New Haven: Yale University Press, 1989.

Hunter, Trent and Stephen Wellum. *Christ from Beginning to End: How the Full Story of Scripture Reveals the Full Glory of Christ.* Grand Rapids, MI: Zondervan, 2018.

James, Carolyn Custis. *Maelstrom: Manhood Swept into the Currents of a Changing World.* Grand Rapids, MI: Zondervan, 2015.

Kottackal, J. "Mary in the Bible." *Bible Bhashyam* 25, no. 2 (1999): 140-41. Accessed August 15, 2017, New Testament Abstracts, EBSCOhost.

Leonard, Jeffery. "Inner-Biblical Interpretation and Intertextuality." In *Literary Approaches to the Bible.* Edited by Douglas Mangum and Douglas Estes, 97-141. Bellingham, WA: Lexham Press, 2017.

Mallen, Peter. *The Reading and Transformation of Isaiah in Luke-Acts.* London: T & T Clark, 2008.

Mayberry, Nancy K. "The 'Strong Woman' in Calderón's *Autos*: The Exegetical and Iconographic Tradition of the Virgin Immaculate." *Bulletin of the Comediantes* 49, no. 2 (1997): 307-18. Accessed June 23, 2018. https://muse.jhu.edu/.

McCann, J. Clinton. *Judges*. Louisville, KY: Westminster John Knox Press, 2011.

Moyise, Steve. "Dialogical Intertextuality." In *Exploring Intertextuality: Diverse Strategies for New Testament Interpretation of Texts*. Edited by B. J. Oropeza and Steve Moyise, 3-15. Eugene, OR: Cascade Books, 2016.

Moyise, Steve. "Intertextuality and Biblical Studies: A Review." *Verbum et Ecclesia 23*, no. 2 (August 2002): 418-31. Accessed June 23, 2018. https://www.researchgate.net/publication/267545243 _Intertextuality_and_Biblical_Studies_A_Review.

Oropeza, B. J. and Steve Moyise, eds. *Exploring Intertextuality: Diverse Strategies for New Testament Interpretation of Texts*. Eugene, OR: Cascade Books, 2016.

McHugh, John. *The Mother of Jesus in the New Testament*. London: Darton, Longman & Todd, 1975.

McKnight, Scot. *The King Jesus Gospel: The Original Good News Revisited*. Grand Rapids, MI: Zondervan, 97.

Pierce, Ronald W. "Deborah: Troublesome Woman or Woman of Valor?" *Priscilla Papers 32*, no. 2 (Spring 2018): 3-7. Accessed June 8, 2018. https://www.cbeinternational.org/sites/default/files/PP322 -pierce.pdf.

Pierce, Ronald W. and Rebecca Merrill Groothuis, eds. *Discovering Biblical Equality: Complementarity Without Hierarchy*. 2nd ed. Downers Grove: IVP Academic, 2005.

Radner, Ephraim. *Hope Among the Fragments: The Broken Church and Its Engagement of Scripture*. Grand Rapids, MI: Brazos Press, 2004.

Ratzinger, Joseph. "The Sign of the Woman: An Introductory Essay on the Encyclical *Redemptoris Mater*." In *Mary, the Church at the*

Source, Joseph Cardinal Ratzinger and Hans Urs von Balthasar, 1-11. San Francisco: Ignatius Press, 2005. Accessed June 23, 2018. http://www.laici.va/content/dam/laici/documenti/ donna/teologia/english/the-sign-of-the-woman-introductory -essay-on-the-encyclical-redemptoris-mater.pdf.

Ronning, John. "John Ronning Seven Keys to the Interpretation of Genesis 3:15." Recording of lecture at Evangelical Theological Society's Eastern Region meeting, April 6-7, 2018. Accessed July 28, 2018. http://www.wordmp3.com/details.aspx?id=27929.

–––––. *The Jewish Targums and John's Logos Theology*. Grand Rapids, MI: Baker Academic, 2010.

Ronning, John L. "The Curse on the Serpent (Genesis 3:15) in Biblical Theology and Hermeneutics." PhD diss., Westminster Theological Seminary, 1997. Accessed September 4, 2017. ProQuest Dissertations Publishing.

Sasson, Jack M. *Judges 1–12*. New Haven: Yale University Press, 2014.

Schreiner, Thomas R. "Foundations for Faith," *The Southern Baptist Journal of Theology* (September 2001): 2-3. Accessed July 21, 2018. http://resources.thegospelcoalition.org/library/editorial -foundations-for-faith.

Trible, Phyllis. *God and the Rhetoric of Sexuality*. Philadelphia: Fortress Press, 1978.

Witherington III, Ben. *Torah Old and New: Exegesis, Intertextuality, and Hermeneutics*. Minneapolis: Fortress Press, 2018.

Wright, Jacob L. "What Gender Issues Are Present in the Book of Judges?" Bible Odyssey. Accessed July 3, 2018. https://www .bibleodyssey.org/tools/video-gallery/g/gender-issues-judges -wright.

Wright, N. T. *Jesus and the Victory of God*. Minneapolis, MN: Fortress Press, 1996.

Younger, K. Lawson, Jr. *Judges and Ruth*. Grand Rapids, MI: Zondervan, 2002.

SCRIPTURE INDEX

(Gen 3:15, Judges 4 and Judges 5 are throughout the text.)

Made in the
USA
Columbia, SC